Eugene B. Weeks

Spiritual Meanings of Biblical Words

Eugene B. Weeks
Spiritual Meanings of Biblical Words
ISBN/EAN: 9783337334888
Printed in Europe, USA, Canada, Australia, Japan
Cover: Foto ©Lupo / pixelio.de

More available books at **www.hansebooks.com**

SPIRITUAL MEANINGS

OF

BIBLICAL WORDS.

By

EUGENE B. WEEKS,
and
CAROLINE S. ALDEN

Chicago:
Published by the School of Christ,
Masonic Temple,
1898.

PREFACE.

In placing this little manual before searchers for the hidden things of Being, more especially as shadowed forth in the Inspired writings of the Bible, we have given expression to an impulse for which we have no excuse, and we trust, for Christ's sake, there shall arise no condemnation in any quarter. Our aim has been to lift up into such terms as should to us suggest the active recognition within us of the divine principles to which the words are self-evidently related.

We make no claim of having reached in every case what might be called interchangeable synonyms, neither have we sought to make this an exhaustive dictionary of Biblical symbology; yet we send forth this little work trusting that many may share with us the joy of unfoldment which it has been to us.

While in the main this is not a compilation, yet in some parts it has been, to us, necessarily so, while in defining a number of words we have seen fit to use the phraseology of other writers along these lines.

We would also acknowledge valuable assistance from Charles G. McKenzie in gleaning and defining words which had escaped our search.

In order to make this appeal to each and all as merely a nucleus for further analysis and unfoldment, we have left ample room for interlineations and marginal additions.

Trusting that to many this little book shall prove a helping hand in bringing to life and light the mysteries of the Kingdom of God as they have been embalmed in the sacred writings of all ages, we send it forth on its mission with a motherly God speed.

                EUGENE B. WEEKS,
                CAROLINE S. ALDEN,
      Directors School of Christ, Chicago.

A

A—Affection, from divine love.

AARON—Teacher, lofty, woman, mountain of strength, enlightened.

AB—Father God. BA—Mother God.

ABAD-DON—Destruction, self-offering.

ABEL—Charity, breath, watchfulness, first fruit.

ABHOR—Utterly swallow up.

ABIDE—Stand firm, rest.

ABIGAIL—My father's joy.

ABOMINATION—Idolatry.

ABOVE—Within, inmost.

ABRAHAM—Father of a multitude, fidelity.

ABRAM—Knowlege of good.

ABROAD—Heaven and earth, all of man, visible and invisible.

ACCEPT—Beloved, grace, favor.

ACCUSER—The dragon.

ACHOR—Trouble.

ACKNOWLEDGMENT—True worship.

ACTION—Effect of love.

ACTIVITIES—Changes or variations of form.

ADAM—Edom, man, red earth.

ADAMANT—Hardness of heart, boldness.

ADD—To destroy, pervert.

ADDER—Evil in general, malice, venom.

ADONIJAH—Perfected man, the strength and power of the two in one.

ADORE—Acknowledge, believe.

ADORN—Radiation of love.

ADOPTION—Receiving the kingdom of God.

ADVENT—Presence of the Lord, the Kingdom of Heaven already come in man, the word made flesh, birth, spiritual and natural.

ADVERSARY—The devil.

ADVOCATE—Illumined reason.

ADULTERY—Attempt to unite truth with error, to corrupt the Word of God, to falsify the truth of man with opinions of the world.

AFAR—Slight unfoldment.

AFFECTION—Love of the truth and fortitude to stand by it.

AFFLICTION—Travail of soul.

AFORE—Prior.

AFRAID—Unbelief.

AFTER—Obey or follow.

AGATE—Love of good.

AGE—Complete state; old age, wisdom.

AGONY—Compelling power of love.

AGRICULTURE—Soul unfolding.

AGRIPPA—Herod.

AHAZ—Possessor.

AI OR HAI—Knowledge of worldly things.

AID OR HELP—Mercy.

AIR—Faith.

ALABASTER—(Onyx) resembling marble.

ALAS—Woe (highest lamentation).

ALIEN—False belief.

ALIVE—That which possesses life, love and truth.

ALLEGORY—Symbolical discourse.

ALLELUIA—Praise Jehovah.

ALLURE—Prove truth through subtle means.

ALMIGHTY—All power, Infinity, able to do all things, Omnipotence.

ALMOND—Interior principle.

ALMS—Exercise of love and justice.

ALOES—External preservation.

ALONE—Only, all, one.

ALPHA—Being, self-existent, love, complete.

ALPHEUS—Chief, a thousand.

ALTAR—Sanctuary of refuge, Christ.

AM—Essence, love.

AMALEK—A people that lick up or take away all.

AMASA—People that forgive.

AMAZED—Signifies acknowledgment.

AMAZIAH—Perverted church.

AMBASSADOR—Messenger.

AMEN—Equals "Aum," the mystic name for Christ.

AMETHYST—Spiritual love of good (Ex. 33: 19).

AMMONITE—Belief in physical causation, materialism.

AMORITE—Evil in general.

AMOS—Burden, weighty.

AMPHITHEATER—Where dragons held their diversions.

ANANIAS—Cloud of the Lord.

ANATHEMA—Outlaw.

ANCHOR—Sure hold-fast.

ANCIENT—Everlasting.

ANDREW—Man, strong, stout.

ANGEL—Man made, messenger.

ANGER—Fear.

ANGLER—Concentration.

ANIMAL—Natural mind.

ANKLE—Sensual or natural.

ANNA—Grace, favor, giver.

ANOINT—Divinely appoint.

ANSWER—Determination, response, unfoldment. Inspiration, perception.

ANT—Industry, providence.

ANTELOPE—Swift-footed.

ANTICHRIST—Adversary to Christ.

ANTIOCH—Speed, as chariot.

ANTIPAS—Confessor of truth.

ANXIETIES—Temptations.

APART—Separate to oneness.

APE—Imitator, imager.

APOSTLE—Teacher, minister sent from Christ.

APOLLOS—One who destroys.

APPAREL—Mental vestment.

APPEARANCE—Presence of.

APPLAUSE—Worship, deification.

APPLE—Seed of God, joy of the heart.

APPOINT—Fixed by God.

APPREHEND—To seize.

APPROACH—Draw near.

APPROVED—Demonstrated.

AQUILA—Eagle.

AR—Awaking, uncovering.

ARABIA—Evening, wild desert.

ARAM—Magnificence.

AR-AR-AT—Holy ground.

ARCHANGEL—Chief angel.

ARCTURUS—An ark.

"ARE"—To be of great value and esteem among men. (1 Cor. 1: 28; Heb. 4: 15; Rev. 1: 19.)

AREOPAGUS—Hill of Mars.

ARETAS—One that pleases.

ARIEL—Lion, hearth of God.

ARIMATHEA—The heights.

ARIOCH—Lion-like.

ARISE—Go to the Source.

ARISTARCHUS—Good chief.

ARM—Infinite power.

ARMAGEDDON—Mountain of Destruction.

ARMOUR—Weapon of defense.

ARMY—Executor of peace.

ARK OF THE COVENANT—Christ, safety, man in God.

ARRAY—Put on apparel.

ARRAYED—Instructed in truth.

ARROW—Judgment.

ART—Attraction, fascination, serpent.

ARTAXERXES—Great warrior, silence of light.

ARTEMAS—Whole.

ASA—Healer.

ASCEND—Go to Source.

ASER—Eternal beatitude.

ASHAMED—In rags of indolence, fatherless.

ASHES—Frailty, humiliation.

ASHNER—Happiness.

ASHORE—Established, manifest.

ASHUR—Rational faculty, hope and faith.

ASIA—Those in the light of truth.

ASK—To realize, pray, communicate, recognize substance.

ASLEEP—Resting in substance or faith.

ASPS—Falsehood that stings to death, sentence pronounced upon man from the standpoint of error.

ASS—Natural man.

ASSEMBLE—To arrange in order.

ASSEMBLY—Presence of the Lord.

ASSURANCE—Certainty.

ASTONISHMENT—Want of perception.

ASTROLOGER—Operation through hope or fear.

AT HAND—Nearness of state.

ATOM—Eternal substance.

ATMOSPHERE—Receptacle of heat and light, sphere of mind.

AT-ONE-MENT—Reception of the Lord, union of God and man, also union of soul and body, through life made visible, which is blood shed, the outflowing life of the Father into man the son.

ATTRACTION—All love.

AUTHORITY—Power derived from faith.

AURORA—Day dawn.

AVARICE—Self-love.

AVENGE—Extinction or destruction.

AWAKE—To rouse up, raise from the dead.

AWL—Affixion.

AXE—Vengeance or judgment of God.
AXIS—Kingdom of heaven in the midst.
AZAL—Separation, liberation.
AZARIAH—Whom the Lord hears.
AZURE—Love of good.

B

B—House, or thought.
BAAL—Self-love, love of the world.
BAALIM—Opinions of the world, Lords many.
BABE—First-born of God.
BABEL, OR BABYLON—Superstition, confusion, profanation of good, kingdom divided against itself.
BACK—Toward Source, again.
BAGS—Receptivity.
BAKE—The truth of doctrine.
BALAAM—Stranger, foreigner, lord of the people.
BALANCE—Estimation of good and truth.
BALM—Sufficient remedy.

BALDNESS—Without proof or demonstration, weak, mean.

BANDS—That which draws or engages a person.

BANNER—Standard, ensign.

BAPTISM—Purification by spirit, saturated with truth, Divine initiation.

BARABBAS—Son of shame, confusion.

BARACHIAS—Who blesses God.

BARBARIAN—Unregenerate man, idol worshiper.

BAR-JESUS—Son of Jesus.

BAR-JONAH—Son of a dove.

BARK—Ultimate of the stem.

BARLEY—Natural good.

BARN OR GRANARY—Heaven. (Matt. 13.)

BARNABAS—Son of exhortation.

BARREN—Denial of being life, truth and love.

BARSABAS—Son of rest.

BARTHOLOMEW—Son that suspends the waters.

BARTIMEUS—Son of the honorable.

BASE—Foundation.

BASHAN—Sandy soil.

BASIN—That which holds truth.

BASKETS—Vessels to contain meat, states of the will.

BATHE—Cleanse with truth.

BATS—Those infatuated with lusts.

BATTLE—Dissension.

BAY TREE—Prosperity.

BDELLIUM, AND THE ONYX STONE—Truth.

BEAR—To carry, bring forth, endure, acknowledge.

BEAR—Power from the natural sense of life, or man.

BEARD—The ultimate of the principle.

BECOME—Enter into recognition, unfold.

BED—State of rest.

BEAST—What is alive, living one.

BEAST—Anti-Christ. (Rev. 13:2.)

BEASTS—Kingdom of God (the four beasts.)

BEATITUDE—Being in God.

BEAUTY—Joy of wholeness.

BEDCHAMBER—Interior of man.

BE—The Lord's presence.

BEE—Reasoning from the principle by the natural man.

BEELZEBUB—Dung-god, the god of falsehood.

BEFORE—First in dignity.

BEGINNING—From be and gynnan, which means to divide, or cut, or split.

BEGOTTEN—Gotten of being in God.

BEGUILE—Led by affections of the flesh.

BEHEMOTH—Elephant, the natural man.

BEHIND—Within, above.

BEHOLD—Perception.

BEING—Eternal life.

BEING—(Esse) prior to form is substance.

BELIAL—Evil or unprofitable spirit.

BELIEF—Confidence.

BELIEVE—"Let be," firm, constant, unfaltering.

BELLS—Sound of truth.

BELLY—Womb, interior, understanding.

BELOVED—The Lord.

BELTSHAZZAR—Divided kingdom.

BENEATH—External, manifestation.

BENEDICTION—Acknowledgment.

BENJAMIN—Innocence of the natural man.

BENONI—Son of my grief.

BERNICE—One that brings victory.

BESIDE—Opposite, reflex.

BETHANY—House of song.

BETHEL—House of God.

BETHESDA—House of mercy.

BETHLEHEM—House of bread.

BETHPHAGE—Place of figs.

BETHSAIDA—House of fruits.

BETRAY—Disclose inner nature or character.

BEYOND—Boundless, infinite.

BILLOWS—Waves of great trial and overwhelming perplexity, doubt and fear.

BIRD—External activity.

BIRTH—Coming forth.

BITTER—Corresponds to falsehood.

BLACK—In the letter, not in the spirit.

BLAMELESS—Holy, pure.

BLASPHEMY—Denial of the Lord.

BLESS—Worship of God.

BLESSED—Immortal.

BLIND—Ignorance of truth.

BLOOD—Holy principle of the body.

BLOSSOM—Receptivity.

BLUE—Faith.

BOANERGES—Highest truths.

BODY—Man (homo).

BONDAGE—State of being, bound by fear or affection.

BONES—Corresponds to substance.

BONNET—Head-covering, intelligence.

BOOK OF LIFE—Record in heaven of man, I am.

BORDER, OR HEM—External or ultimate of principle.

BORE—Obedience.

BORN OF GOD—Principled in love.

BOSOM, OR BREAST—Spiritual love.

BOTTLE—The mind of man.

BOTTOM—Principle, basis.

BOUGHS—The good of truth.

BOUGHT—Called of God.

BOW—To humble, to rejoice, victory.

"BOW IN THE CLOUD"—Regeneration.

BOWELS—Essential love.

BOX TREE—Understanding of good and truth.

BOZRAH—Vintage, Edom, Adam, truth.

BRAIN—Corresponds to mental receptivity.

BRAMBLE—Spurious good.

BRANCH—Affection of love.

BRAND—Sign of possession, regenerate body.

BRASS—Immovability, hardness.

BRAZEN SERPENT—Divine humanity of the Lord.

BREACH—Separation, false doctrine.

BREAD—The Lord himself.

BREADTH—The truth of the church.

BREAK—Annihilate.

BREASTPLATE—Divine truth.

BREATH—God's powerful word.

BRETHREN—Affection of truth, life, and love.

BRICK—False or artificial.

BRIDE AND BRIDEGROOM—Purity and innocence, perfected man in God, spiritual understanding.

BRIDE-CHAMBER—Illumined mentality.

BRIDLE—Moral restraint.

BRIERS AND THORNS—False beliefs and
BRIMSTONE—Filthy lusts.
opinions of men.

BRING—The presence of.

BROIDERED WORK—Genuine application of truth.

BROKEN—Doctrine of separation in all its aspects.

BROOK—Tributary to truth.

BROW—Intellectual proceeding.

BRUISE—Chastise, correct.

BUCKLER—Defense.

BUD—First sign of re-birth.

BUILD—To raise up, to instruct.

BULLS—Fierce enemies.

BULWARKS—Truths.

BURDEN—The word.

BURIAL—Submerged in spirit, immortality brought to life.

BURNT OFFERING—Love offering, obedience.

BURY—Return to bosom of mother, resolve into principle.

BUSH—Self-evident truth.

BUSINESS—Activities of spiritual life.

BUTTER AND HONEY—The Lord's delight in conscious being.

BUTTERFLIES—Confirmation of unfoldment.

BUY—Procure, redemption.

C

CAIN—Faith without love.

CAESAR—King of mortal beliefs.

CAKE—Good which nourishes.

CALAMITY—Blighted fruitage.

CALEB—A basket.

CALF—Affection of knowing truth.

CALLED—Chosen of God.

CALM—Poise, living repose.

CALVARY—Place of skulls, intellectuality.

CAME—The beginning.

CAMEL—Scientific knowledge.

CAMELS' HAIR—The ultimate of scientific knowledge.

CAMP—Orderly unfoldment.

CANA OF GALILEE—Mental activities, zeal of the individual.

CANAAN—He that subdues.

CANDLE—Divine favor, grace.

CANDLESTICK—New creature.

CAPERNAUM—Repentance, comfort.

CHILD—Visible word, word made flesh, manifest Father-Mother God in maturity.

CHILDREN OF ISRAEL—Seed of God, representations of substance, offspring of Father-Mother.

CHOOSE—Appoint, act of God, ordain.

CHORAZIN—Secret, mystery.

CHRIST—Son of God, annointed one.

CHRISTIAN—One who embodies God's idea of man.

CHURCH—Assembly, structure of truth and love.

CIRCLE—Heaven.

CIRCUMCISION—Purity.

CISTERN—Natural mind.

CITIZEN—State in consciousness, problem of life.

CITY—Seat of power.

CLAY—Adam, plastic nature.

CLEAN—Free from sin.

CLIMATE—Change of state.

CLOAK—Exterior truth.

CLOSET—Bosom of the Father, secret place of the most high.

CLOTHE—Instruct in truth.

CLOUDS—Veiled glory, majesty.

COALS—Burning love.

COAST—Idea of being.

COAT—Interior truth.

COCKATRICE—Evil imagery.

COCK-CROWING—Twilight, morning.

COLD—No love.

COLOR—Character.

COMB—Logic, reason.

COME—Draw nigh, arise, execute judgment.

COMFORTER—Divine truth.

COMMANDMENT—Word of God.

COMMON—Natural, unproven.

COMMUNION—Concord, fellowship, agreement, atonement.

COMPASSION—Love, mercy.

COMPANY—Assembly.

COMPEL—Action of love.

CONCEIVE—Bear, bring forth, acknowledgment.

CONCEPTION—First reception of truth.

CONCUBINAGE—Apart from the wife.

CONDEMNATION—Judgment less than perfection and wholeness.

CONFESS THE LORD—To be as he is.

CONFIDENCE—Security, certainty by faith.

CONFIRM—To prove, strengthen.

CONFOUND—Baffle, confute.

CONQUER—Overcome, rise above.

CONSCIENCE—Secret judgment.

CONSCIOUSNESS—Being revealed to Being, the house, the temple, the arena of universal operations and government.

CONSECRATE—Set apart.

CONSIDER—Study, resolve, determine.

CONSOLATION—Inward peace and comfort.

CONSUMING—All-absorbing.

CONTEND—Strive.

CONTINUAL—All in all.

CONVERSION—Turned toward the truth.
CONVICTION—Faith, self-evidence.
CO-OPERATE—Work with God.
COPPER—Natural good.
CORDS—Conjunction of God and man.
CORINTH—Ornament, beauty.
CORN—Reception and increase, cheerfulness.
CORNER-STONE—The principal stone (chief element), I am.
CORNELIUS—Of the sun.
CORNET—Trumpet.
CORRESPONDENCE—The invisible appearing in the visible.
CORRUPT—Destitute.
CORRUPTIBLE—Without substance.
COUNCIL—Meeting of the three in one.
COUNSEL—Advice, will, design.
COUNTENANCE—Presence, love and glory.
COUNTRY—State of being.
COURAGE—Fortitude, faith.
COURT—External of the word.

COVENANT—Agreement, marriage, atonement.

COVER—Overshadow.

COVET—Want that which you have not.

COW—Natural principle.

CREATION—Work of Creator.

CREATOR—Self-existent life, truth, love, Son in the bosom of the Father, the Lord.

CRIMSON—Spiritual good.

CRIPPLE—Of feeble understanding.

CROCODILE—Guileful, deceitful.

CROSS—Blending of God and man, true lifting up from the earth.

CROW, OR RAVEN—Thick darkness from false beliefs.

CROWN—Victory through embodying life.

CRUCIFY—Deny, blaspheme, condemn, curse.

CRY—Extending the voice by intense heartbreak.

CRYSTAL—Divine truth.

CUBIT—Quality.

CUCUMBER—The lowest natural, or sensual.

CUNNING—Crafty.

CUP—Measure, the truth of faith.

CURE—Restoration to spiritual life, perfect wholeness.

CURSE—Condemn.

CURTAINS—Truths proceeding from God.

CUT—Separate, divide.

CUT WOOD—To believe in doing before being.

CYMBAL—Joy of heart.

CYPRUS—Fair.

CYRUS—Sun, splendor.

D

DAGGER—False doctrine.

DAGON—Fish, swimmer.

DAILY—Perpetual.

DAMARIS—Maiden.

DAMASCUS—Industry, busy place.

DAMNATION—Self-destruction.

DAMSEL—That which imbibes truth.

DAN—Judge, one belief chasing another.

DANCES—Pleasantness, joy.

DANIEL—God's judge.

DARIUS—Preserver.

DARKNESS—Ignorance, unbelief, hatred, sin.

DARTS—Sudden temptations.

DATES—Good of faith.

DAUGHTER—Divine idea and its affection.

DAVID—Dear, beloved.

DAWN—Birth or coming forth.

DAY—Light, judgment, irradiance of life.

DAY-SPRING—Christ, the Lord.

DEAF—Not in understanding of truth.

DEAL—Operate with.

DEARLY BELOVED—Blessed.

DEATH—True lifting up from the earth.

DEBASED—Disreputable among men.

DEBORAH—Word.

DEBT—Conjunction, charity between man and man.

DECALOGUE—The law.

DECAPOLIS—Ten cities.

DECEIT—Falsehood, good and evil.

DECLARE—Flow in, make known.

DECLINE—Disappear, refuse.

DECORATE—Ornament.

DECORUM—Good form.

DECREE—Act of judgment.

DEDICATE—Set apart.

DEED—Effect of thought.

DEEP—Inmost.

DEER—Affection for truth.

DEFENSE—Salvation, protection.

DEFILE—Adulterate.

DEFY—Stand on principle.

DEGREES—Unfoldment in truth.

DELIGHT—Satisfaction.

DELIVER—Set free.

DELUGE—Truth destroying falsehood.

DEMON—Perverted judgment.

DEMONSTRATION—Unfoldment, proof.

DEN—Habitation, dark dwelling place.

DENARIUS—Penny.

DENY—Shut out, fail to embody.

DEPART—Recede.

DESCEND—Unfold, come forth.

DESERT—Secret chambers.

DESIRE—Seek of truth.

DESOLATE—Separated in belief from God.

DESPAIR—Restrained desire.

DESPISE—Spurn, turn away from.

DESTROY—Devastate, demolish.

DETERMINE—Appoint, fix, set.

DEVICE—Plan, scheme.

DEVIL—Self-love, personal belief of evil.

DEVOUR—Read and embody.

DEW—Divine blessing.

DIADEM—Crown, ornament for the head.

DIAMOND—Truth, spiritual light.

DIANA—Perfect, luminous.

DIBON—Understanding.

DID—Worked out, performed.

DIDYMUS—A twin.

DIG—Discover, or uncover.

DIE—Giving up and going away from the false belief of life, true lifting up from the earth.

DILIGENT—Watchful, concentrated.

DINNER—Feast of love, life, truth, communion.

DIP—Defile, mix or adulterate.

DISCIPLE—True worshiper, instructed by the Lord.

DISCORD—Opposition, chaos.

DISCOVER—Reveal, uncover.

DISEASE—Want, unrest.

DISH—Cup, measure.

DISHONOR — Immaterial, unworthy of praise.

DISMAY—Fear, uncertainty.

DISMOUNT—Return to common-place or animal plane.

DISOBEDIENT—Refractory, stubborn.

DISTANT—Remote, dissimilar in some degree.

DITCH—False opinion or doctrine.

DIVERSITY—Infinite things in God-man.

DIVES—Jews, self-love.

DIVIDED—Unholy, destroyed.

DIVINATION—Witchcraft.

DIVINE—Of God and his idea.

DIVISIONS—Searchings, trying the heart and reins.

DIVORCE—Putting away.

DO—Action of mind.

DOCTOR—Teacher of truth, doer of the Word.

DOG—Contempt, impurity, ungodly person.

DOMINION—Rule, authority.

DONE—Finished, consummated.

DOOR—Communion, entrance, truth, the Lord.

DOORPOSTS—Uprightness of the Lord.

DOUBLE—Fulfill, externalize or make manifest.

DOUBT—Uncertainty.

DOVE—Holy Spirit, purity, man as he is in God.

DOWN—Out, revealed.

DRAGON—Cruelty, false teacher.

DRAW—Make as one.

DREAD—Reverence.

DREAM—Ideal, image.

DRINK—Appropriate, solve in truth, make clear.

DRIVE—Force by self-evidence.

DROMEDARY—Knowledge of truth.

DROPS—Divine intelligence.

DROSS—The worthless element.

DROUGHT—Deprive of truth.

DRUNKENNESS—Infatuation.

DRY GROUND—Love extinguished.

DUMB—Cannot confess the Lord or truth of being.

DUNG—Utter contempt.

DUNGEON—Dark pit or den, prison.

DUST—Humility.

DWELL—To possess, inhabit, to be in the presence of.

E

E—Means love, the Lord.

EAGLE—Power, strength of principle.

EARLY—Quickly, clearly.

EARNEST—Fruit of the spirit, assurance.

EARRINGS—Obedience to truth.

EARS—Understanding, perception.

EARTH—Mother, man, formed word, compound idea.

EARTHQUAKE—Change of state.

EASE—Rest, heaven.

EAST—Jehovah himself, day dawn.

EAST WIND—Destruction of error, dispersion of falsehood.

EAT—Communion, conjunction, appropriation.

EBAL—Unfruitful.

EBENEZER—Stone of help.

EBER—Passer over.

ECCLESIASTES—Preacher.

EDGE—Cutting point, mouth, separation.

EDEN—Edom, man including woman, blessedness, immortality.

EDIFY—To please or instruct in truth.

EDOM—The word made flesh, truth of the natural man.

EFFECT—Result, fruit, body.

EGG—Type of resurrection, age of infancy.

EGLAIM—Drops of the sea.

EGYPT—Woman, mother, earth, darkness

EGYPTIAN—Natural science, servant.

EIGHT—Transfiguration, fullness, regeneration, beginning of a new state.

EIGHTEEN THOUSAND—Uncompromising truth.

EL—God in will and act.

ELAM—Eternity.

EL-BETHEL—Resting in truth.

ELDERS—Traditions of the fathers.

ELDERS—(Twenty-four; Rev. 4: 4)—Spiritual unfoldment, knowledge of truth.

ELEAZAR—God my helper, court of God.

ELECT—Set apart, appointed of God.

ELEMENTS—Divine characteristics, food of the mind.

ELEPHANT—Natural man.

ELEVEN—State of reception.

ELI—My God, lifting up, lofty.

ELIAB—Father of the father, God of the father.

ELIAKIM—God raises.

ELIAS—Self-evidence, true prophecy.

ELIHU—God is he.

ELIM—Trees, rest.

ELIJAH—Strong God.

ELIZABETH—The oath of God.

ELM—(Same as oak)—Strength.

ELOHIM—Truths in conjunction, plural of El.

ELOQUENCE—Joy of mind.

ELYMAS—Corrupter.

EMBALM—Sanctify in truth.

EMBASSADOR—Sent of the Lord.

EMBODY—Invest with form.

EMBRACE—Embody with love.

EMBROIDER—Interweavings of truth in man.

EMERALDS—Knowledge of good, appearance of the Divine.

EMERODS—Self-love.

EMMANEUL—God with us. (Emma means with, nu means us; El means God.)

EMMAUS—Hot springs.

EMPTY—Nothing, void.

ENCAMP—Arrange in divine order.

ENCHANTMENT—Magical charm.

ENCOMPASS—Protection of God, limitation of men.

ENCOURAGED—Strengthened, uplifted.

END—Result, effect, word made form or flesh.

ENDURANCE—Faith.

ENEAS—Praise.

ENEMIES—Worldly belief and opinion, traditions of men.

ENGEDI—Fountain of truth.

ENGLAIM—Love of truth.

ENGRAVER—Finger of God.

ENJOY—Being alive in truth.

ENLIGHTENED—Illumined.

ENMITY—Opposed to good.

ENOCH—Dedicated, initiated.

ENOS—Mortal man.

ENOUGH—All in all.

ENQUIRE—Ask, pray, desire, realize by faith.

ENSIGN—Son of man.

ENTER—Living at-onement, communication.

ENTERTAIN—Consider without prejudice.

ENTICE—Tempt, allure with appearances.

ENTRANCE—I am the door.

ENTREAT—Drawing power of love.

ENVY—Work of darkness or ignorance.

EPHAH—Much, quality of reception.

EPHESUS—Defense.

EPHOD—Perfect external, garment of righteousness.

EPHRAIM—Double fruitfulness, twin-land.

EPHRATAH—Fruitful.

EPISTLE—Written word.

EQUAL—One, all, whole.

EQUIP—Make complete.

EQUITY—Justice, judgment.

ER—Man in the original; also means, to kill or beat.

ERASTUS—Amiable, lovely.

ERE—Before.

ERROR—Adverse.

ESAU—Hairy, doing without knowledge of being.

ESCAPE—Liberation, become free.

ESCHOL—Bunch of grapes.

ESSE—Being, source.

ESSENCE—One, unadulterated.

ESTABLISHED—Set up, fixed.

ESTATE—Inheritance, eternal life.

ESTEEM—Value, recognize, love.

ESTHER—Hidden sweets.

ETERNAL—Everlasting, age-lasting, without beginning or end, endless, ceaseless.

ETHAN—Strong.

ETHIOPIA—Burning.

EUNICE—Victory.

EUNUCH—One who guards truth, servant of truth.

EUPHRATES—That which makes fruitful, the true idea of God in man.

EUROCLYDON—Northeast wind.

EUTYCHUS—Fortunate.

EVE—Life at-one with love, the mother of all living, the be-ginning.

EVEN, EVENING—Blending, uniting, harmonizing.

EVER—At all times.

EVERYONE—All.

EVIDENCE—Basis of belief or judgment.

EVIL—Result of judging by appearances only.

EWE-LAMB—Holiness of innocence.

EXACT—Correct, accurate, perfect.

EXAMINE—Repent, test by law, tried by fire.

EXALT—Worship, extol.

EXAMPLE—Model, out-picture of idea.

EXCEEDING—Passing beyond.

EXCELLENCY—State of perfection.

EXCEPT—Unless.

EXCHANGE—Instead, in place of.

EXCLUDE—Leave out.

EXCUSE—Apology, acknowledgment of other gods.

EXECUTE—Work out, perform.

EXERCISE—To practice, to use, to keep employed.

EXHORT—Entice by word, or stimulate to execution.

EXILE—Banished from the soul as offensive.

EXISTENCE—Life-action related to life.

EXODUS—Going to the Father, proceeding forth in soul unfoldment, seed going to seed.

EXPECTATION—Looking to that which is.

EXPEDIENT—Profitable, necessary.

EXPERIENCE—Result of knowledge, effect of being.

EXPERT—Skillful, disciplined, adroit.

EXPLORE—To unfold.

EXPOSE—Lay open, uncover.

EXPOUND—Set forth, explain.

EXPRESS—Declare, make known.

EXTEND—Bring forth into action.

EXTERNAL—Exists from and has body from the internal.

EXTINGUISH—Quench, being at an end.

EXTOL—Praise.

EYE—Perception, knowledge.

EYELIDS—Truth is its own protection.

EYE SERVANTS—Living witnesses.

EZEKIEL—Strength of God.

EZIONGEBER—Giant's backbone.

EZRA—Help.

F

F—Means "Let there be," perfected man.

FABLE—Instructive story to enforce truth.

FACE—Visible presence, corresponds to mercy, peace; eyes understanding, nose perception, ears obedience, mouth desire for wisdom, forehead the good of love, and intellectual things of men, chin will, right cheek affection, left cheek understanding.

FACULTY—Power of mind, dual as will and understanding.

FADE—Vanish.

FAIL—Not to be, deficient.

FAINT—To be without substance, or without life or faith.

FAIR—Wise.

FAITH—Self-evidence, confidence, knowledge, substance, Father Almighty.

FALL—Deception, falsehood.

FALLACY—Opinions, theories, speculations.

FALLOW-GROUND—Good and honest heart.

FALSE—Untrue, counterfeit.

FAME—Renown, vanity.

FAMILY—Father-mother-child.

FAMINE—Rejection of life.

FAN—Separation of falsehood from truth.

FAR—Apart, separated from, a great degree removed.

FARE—To feed, satisfaction and delight in truth, state of being.

FARTHING—(To pay the uttermost), is to be punished to the fullest extent.

FASHION—Custom, to form or make.

FASTING—Abstaining from falsehood.

FAT—Highest principle, goodness, father.

FATE—Destiny, predetermined end seen from beginning.

FATHER—Father-Mother, Source, the Begetter, substance.

FATLINGS—Delights of affection.

FATNESS—Perpetual fountain of love, life, truth.

FAULT—Missing the mark, blemish, puzzled.

FAVOR—Grace, love.

FEAST—Worship of the Lord.

FEAR—Reverence, veneration, love, dread, to regard in consciousness.

FEATHERS—Spiritual good, honor.

FEEBLE—Lack of life and truth.

FEED—To teach.

FEEL—The affection of realized good.

FEELING—Perception externalized.

FEET—Natural principle, understanding, foundation.

FELIX—Happy.

FELLOW—Companion, an equal, one of a pair.

FEMALE—Double of male.

FERMENT—Leaven, that which raises or lifts.

FERVENT—Ardor of divine love.

FESTUS—Joyful.

FEVER—Shuddering, agitation.

FEW—Two or three, one, I and my Father.

FIAT—Decree, command.

FIDELITY — Veracity, firm, adherence, faith.

FIELD—Doctrine, the world, the church.

FIERY—Born of divine love, fierce, zealous.

FIFTY—Eternal life, the year of jubilee, liberty to captives.

FIG TREE—Woman; fruit of the fig tree, type of the word demonstrated.

FIG-TREE (BARREN) — Works without faith, exuberance of leaves, doctrines, without substance. (The Jesus in man is always hungry for the fruit of the Spirit. Being before doing.)

FIGHT—Unfolding of the soul to itself (same as birth).

FILL—Being all in all, being eternal life.

FILTHY—Self-loves.

FIND—Discover, to enjoy, determine, to be.

FINGER OF GOD—Power terminating in the ultimate.

FINE—Clear, pure, perfect.

FINISHED—At-one with the Father.

FINITE—External, effect, result, finished, end.

FIR TREE—"To a point," that which relates to the Kingdom of God.

FIRE—Our God, Love.

FIRM—Fixed, set, steadfast.

FIRMAMENT—Internal man, wide extent, expanse.

FIRST—All, the Lord.

FIRST-BEGOTTEN, FIRST-BORN—Truth in act and operation, man, the Lord.

FIRST FRUIT—Seed.

FISH—Jesus Christ, God in action.

FISHER—One who searches out and teaches the truth of man in God.

FIT—Suitable, becoming.

FIVE—Law of being, the commandment, God said, "Let there be."

FIX—State of holy love, rest.

FLAGS—Banners, ensigns, statements of truth.

FLAME—Effect of fire, beloved one, appearance of love.

FLATTERERS—Double-minded.

FLAX—Spiritual truth, (to make and weave flax signifies to teach).

FLEA—Annoying suggestion.

FLEE—To escape.

FLEECE—Calm radiation of right-mindedness.

FLESH—Divine humanity, the truth of life.

FLESH-POTS—Beliefs and opinions, falsehoods, superstitions.

FLIES—Ill will, sensuality.

FLIGHT—Spiritual unfoldment.

FLINT—Truths.

FLOCK—Interior truth.

FLOOD—Reasonings grounded in principle, truths from truth.

FLOOR—That which is laid or spread.

FLOUR—Principle of love, the truth of faith.

FLOURISH—Multiply, enlarge, unfold.

FLOW—Issue, to proceed, glide into.

FLOWERS—The rebirth of man.

FLY—Omnipresence, foresee, provide.

FOAL—Humility and affection of natural man.

FOES—That which opposes principle, the adversary.

FOLDS—Bosom of the Father, place of security.

FOLK—Mental situations, problems.

FOLLOW THE LORD—To be as he is, acknowledge in all ways.

FOLLY—Ignorance, want of knowledge or understanding.

FOOD—That which nourishes and sustains both soul and body.

FOOL—Self-derived intelligence.

FOOT—Fundamental principle.

FOOTSTOOL—Visible church.

FORCE—Father-Son-Holy Spirit.

FOREFATHERS—Foreshadowings of the Kingdom.

FOREHEAD—Heavenly love, overshadowing of love, "written upon the forehead," implanted in love.

FOREIGNER—One who acts from and for self only, stranger to truth.

FOREKNOW—Conceive, beget.

FORE-ORDAIN—The end seen in the beginning.

FORESKIN—(circumcision of)—Re-membering the perfect source.

FOREST—Natural man.

FORGET—To lose consciousness, neglect, let go of.

FORGIVE—Pardon, give for, render life for life, truth for truth, etc.

FORM—Essence or substance of a thing.

FORMER—From the beginning.

FORNICATION—Idolatry.

FORSAKE—Withdraw from, leave.

FORSWEAR—Perjure before Christ Jesus.

FORTITUDE—Firmness.

FORTUNATUS—Lucky.

FORTUNE—Eternal life, the gift of God.

FORWARD—Action through faith, soul-unfoldment.

FORTY—Complete state, existence.

FOUND—Being in God.

FOUNDATION—Ground-work, basis.

FOUNTAIN—Source, cause, the Lord.

FOUR—Justice, the double of two, visible witness.

FOUR BEASTS (seen by Daniel)—Successive states of the church.

FOURFOLD—Son of God seen in Son of man.

FOWLS OF THE AIR—Mental activities.

FOX—Crafty, cunning, sly.

FRAGMENTS — Knowledges and perceptions of truth.

FRAGRANCE—Affection of truth.

FRAILTY—Seen from without, or as expression.

FRAME—Form, law, constructiveness.

FRANK—Candid, generous.

FRANKINCENSE—Spiritual good, praise and true prayer.

FRAUD—Opinions, beliefs, traditions.

FREE—Unreserved, unconstrained.

FREEDOM—Liberty, to will and do as the Father.

FREE WILL—Divine action.

FRIEND—Brother, sister, mother, man in God.

FRIENDSHIP—Bond between God and man.

FRINGES—Externals, speech.

FROGS—Croakers, mutterers.

FRONT—In judgment.

FRONTLETS—Understanding.

FROST—Truth in the form of good, rigidity of truth.

FROTH—Evil, false.

FRUCTIFY—To make fruitful, or render productive.

FRUIT—Effect, first fruit is faith, seed, the work of God.

FRUITFUL—Multiplied in truth.

FRUITFUL ONE—Mother, the good of love.

FRUIT-TREE—Man.

FUGITIVE—Stranger to truth.

FULFILLED—Finished, complete.
FULL—Perfect before God.
FULLNESS OF TIMES—When the Lord appears.
FUNCTIONS—Spiritual activities.
FURLONGS—Leading truths.
FURNACE—Natural man.
FURROWS—Stirrings of the Holy One.
FURY—Violence, vengeance.
FUTURE—Expansion of to-day, unfoldment of now.
FY—Contempt.

G

GABRIEL—Strength of God, lip of God, mouth of God, man of God.
GAD—Omnipotence, good fortune, good works.
GAIN—False judgment.
GALBANUM—Gum used in incense.
GALILEE—Wheel, revolution. ("I come from the Father and go to the Father").

GALEED—Heap, witness.

GALL—Infernal falsity.

"GALL AND WORMWOOD"—Good and evil.

GARDEN—Man natural.

GARDEN AND PARADISE—Intellect and wisdom.

GARDEN EASTWARD IN EDEN—The Lord.

GARDENER—Doing on the external plane, action.

GARMENT—Understanding, word, divine truth.

GARNER, OR GRANARY OR BARN—Heaven within you.

GARNISHED—Harmonious in feeling.

GATE—I am, doctrine, word, entrance, door, way.

GATH—Wine press.

GATHER—To remember.

GAVE—Sent forth, made, manifest.

GAZA—Strong.

GAZE—Meditate, be receptive to the Word.

GEHENNA—Place of burning.

GEMS—Truths unadulterated.

GENEALOGY—States of unfoldment.

GENERATE—To form.

GENERATION—Unfolding of me to myself.

GENESARETH—Knowledge of truth.

GENESIS—Alpha and Omega, beginning in which is the end.

GENII—Based in falsehood.

GENITALS—Union of good and truth.

GENIUS—Unfolding of Christ.

GENTILES—Those in darkness who accept the word readily.

GENTLE—Compassionate, kind.

GERMINATION—Production of wisdom and love.

GESTURES—Affections of love.

GET—Being, be.

GETHSEMANE—The expansion of soul in patience.

GHOST—Breath of life, holy guest, spirit.

GIANTS—Love of self separate from God.

GIBEAH—Hill, heap.

GIBEON—Cup, lifted up, desiring knowledge for personal good.

GIFT—My lot in God, the Kingdom of God.

GIHON—Intuition, that which flows down from the mother.

GILDED—Pretentious, hypocritical, acquired good.

GILEAD—Good of faith, self-evidence.

GILGAL—Natural truth.

GINS—Deception, enticement.

GIRD ONE'S SELF—To know the truth.

GIRDLE OR ZONE—Common band, doctrine of the word.

GIRGASHITE, AND JEBUSITE—Pilgrims and sojourners.

GIRLS AND BOYS—Mind and idea in its innocence.

GIVE—To lay up treasure in heaven.

GLAD—Joy of heart.

GLASS—Wisdom of love.

GLEAN—To follow teachers, search for the substance.

GLORIFY—Celebrate the truth by being it.

GLORY—The Lord and His unfoldment, in light.

GNASHING OF TEETH—Individual disputations.

GO—Be, proceed in the order of Being.

GOAT—Natural man, the worthless.

GOBLETS—Receptacles of truth.

GOD—Unseen, unknown, unnamed One.

GODS—Idols, mythology.

GOG AND MAGOG—Worship in the letter only.

GOLD—Highest spiritual good, purity.

GOLD TRIED IN THE FIRE—Good of celestial love.

GOLDEN AGE—Innocence and integrity.

GOLDEN ALTAR—The Lord.

GOLDEN CALF—Pleasure of the world.

GOLDSMITH—Wise man.

GOLGOTHA—Skulls.

GOLIAH—Giant of intellectualism, pride of worldly wisdom.

GOLIATH—Passage, expeller.

GOMER—External worship.

GOMORRAH—Rebellious people, people that fear.

GOOD—Flowing in of life, truth and love, God.

GOOD OF LOVE—The presence of love.

GOOD OF TRUTH—Embodied truth.

GOOD-WILL—God's will and testament.

GOOSE—Mortal sense.

GOPHER WOOD—Indestructible substance.

GOSHEN—The inmost of the natural mind.

GOSPEL—Glad tidings, God-spell, Christ Jesus.

GOTTEN—Acquired.

GOURD—Grass, self-love.

GOVERNMENT—Power in One.

GRACE—Favor, love, nature of God.

GRAIN—Interior good.

GRANARY—Heaven.

GRANT—Allow, realize.

GRAPE—Fruit of truth, life eternal.

GRASS—First springing forth of the Word, blade.

GRASSHOPPER—Locust, destroyer.

GRAVE—Adam, darkness, cave, soil, or soul before it proves itself.

GRAVEN IMAGE—Self-derived intelligence.

GRAVITY—That which draws to the Father.

GREAT—Marvelous.

GREECE—External beauty.

GREEN (like the emerald)—What is alive, man in God, feminine principle.

GREY HAIR—Honor.

GRIEF—Anxiety of heart.

GRIND—Collect and learn that which is from faith.

GRINDERS—Principles of truth.

GRIZZLED—Good and evil.

GROAN—Dissatisfaction with less than holiness.

GROUND—Infinite mind, the church of God.

GROVE—Intelligence.

GROW—Unfold from perfection to perfection.

GUARD—Store up, watch that which is.

GUILE—Seduce, falsify.

GUILTY—Unrestrained in worldly belief.

GULF—Separation from.

GUSH—Swift action of truth.

H

H—Infinity, esse, I am, divinity. (It gives strength to any letter to which it is joined.)

HA—Surprise, joy.

HAB-AK-KUK—Embraces.

HABITATION—Life.

HADES—Darkness, mystery, death.

HAGAR—One that fears, a stranger, flight.

HAGGAI—Feast, turning around.

HAI, OR AI—Heap of ruins, light derived from worldly things.

HAIL—Destruction.

HAIL (joyful salutation)—Thou art holy, or whole.

HAIR—Natural principle, the ultimate of wisdom.

HAIRY GARMENT—Natural truth.

HALF—The double.

HALL—Mental situation, place of judgment.

HALLELUIAH—The praise of God.

HALLOWED—Holy, the Father hallows His name in man, man hallows his name in God.

HALO—Sphere of divine good.

HALT—Delusion of the senses.

HAM—The church destroyed, literal sense of the word, personal belief.

HAMAN—Alone.

HAMMER—Faith in the ultimate.

HAMOTH—Defense.

HAND—Ability, power, confidence, efficiency.

HANDIWORK—Creative power.

HAND-MAID—Affirmation of good.

HANDLES—Faculty of conjunction with good.

HANG—To reject.

HANNAH—Gracious, giver.

HANNOCH—Dedicated.

HAPPEN—Dispensation under the law, unfoldment.

HAPPINESS—Effect of the spirit, fruit of immortality.

HAPPY—Blessed, immortal.

HARAN—Idolatrous worship, enclosed.

HARBOR—Haven, rest in truth.

HARD SAYING—Not understood.

HARLOT—False affection, church corrupted.

HARMONY—Embodiment of love.

HARP—Confession of the Lord from love and joy of heart.

HARROW—Deposit in the memory.

HARSHNESS—Literal sense of the Word.

HART—Natural affection of truth.

HARVEST—Increase in the perfected Word, ingathering.

HASTEN—What is certain, also what is full, what is quick, alive.

HATCH—To unfold in uses.

HATCHET—Ax, true intelligence.

HATE—To be adverse to.

HATRED—Fountain of all iniquity.

HAUGHTY—Vainly puffed up, mighty in worldly wisdom.

HAVE—The ultimate of being or judgment, manifest substance, conviction, effect.

HAVILAH—Celestial man, passover.

HAWK—Natural man, in belief, separate from God.

HAZOR—Knowledge of truth.

HE—Jehovah.

HEAD—The Word, love and wisdom.

HEALING—I am, the Lord.

HEAP—Altar of God.

HEAR—To understand and embody truth, obedience from affection.

HEART—Vital principle, life, truth, love in one.

HEAT—Infinities of God's love, zeal.

HEATHEN—Those out of the knowledge of being life.

HEAVEN—The throne of the Lord, atmosphere of the soul, perfect union of soul and body.

HEAVY—Falsehood, laden with evils of all kinds.

HEBREW—Interior man.

HEBRON—Enchantment, inclosure, conjunction.

HEDGE—Preservation, salvation, wall.

HEEL—Natural things of the lowest order, corporeal.

HEIFER—Innocence of the external man, which is in ignorance.

HEIGHT—That which towers above all things, altitude, elevation.

HEIR—Entitled to God's throne, or the Kingdom of God.

HELL—Where nothing is seen, place of the dead, all that maketh and worketh a lie.

HELMET—Divine truth.

HELP-MEET—Bone of my bone, flesh of my flesh.

HEM—Natural principles.

HEMLOCK—Unpleasantness.

HEN—Mother love, protection that provides and shelters.

HENCE—From now, and here.

HEP-ZI-BAH—My delight in her.

HERB—The unfolding of truth in some phase.

HERD—External manifestation.

HEREDITARY—All things delivered unto me by my Father.

HERESIES—Falsities that arise from worldly opinions, judging by appearances.

HERITAGE—Substance of the Father.

HERMAS—Refuge.

HERMON—Mountain peak.

HEROD—Glory of the skin.

HERODIAS—Proud place.

HETH—Trembling or fear.

HEWERS OF WOOD—Good works, works without faith in being.

HEZEKIAH—Might of Jehovah.

HIDDEKEL—Reasoning from being, from cause to effect.

HIDE—Concealed, to be invisible.

HIDE OR SKIN—External truth.

HI-ERAPOLIS—Holy city.

HIGGAION—Harmony, meditation.

HIGH—Inmost, heaven.

HIGHEST—Man in God.

HIGH-PRIEST—Divine good.

HIGH-WAY — Way of wholeness. Jesus Christ.

HILLS—The good of love.

HIM—The Lord.

HIND—Natural affection.

HINGE—Governing principle.

HINNON—Riches of the world.

HIRAM—Noble.

HIRE—The Lord unfolding Himself to Himself, my reward is with me.

HISS—Condemn.

HITHERTO—Every time till now.

HITTITE—Envy, belief of separation, who is broken.

HIVITE—Lechery, idolatry.

HO—Be still, look up.

HOARFROST—Truth in the form of good.

HOBAD—Beloved.

HOGS—Avarice and its delights.

HOLD—Den, dungeon, confinement.

HOLINESS—Uprightness and judgment, perfection.

HOLY—Whole, complete, glorified with God.

HOLY CITY—The Lord from heaven, mother of us all.

HOLY OF HOLIES—The inmost heaven.

HOLY SPIRIT—Life-truth-love, embodied in one.

HOLY SUPPER—Eating my flesh, drinking my blood.

HOMER—Measure, sufficient quantity.

HOME—Native harmony, heaven, perfect unison of soul and body.

HONESTY—True to truth.

HONEY—Delight in the Lord, sweetness of the Word, pleasantness from understanding truth.

HONEYCOMB AND BROILED FISH—Use of the word and the truth of it combined.

HONOR—Worship, revere, adore, glorify.

HOOF—Truth in ultimate degree, sensual.

HOOK IN THE NOSE—Stupidity, foolishness.

HOPE—Radiation of faith, experience of faith.

HOBAB—Beloved.

HOREB—The good of love shining forth in divine law.

HORN—Omnipotence, power in speaking, teaching, and writing.

HORNETS—Falsities of a tormenting and destructive kind.

HORROR—Intensified fear.

HORSE—Knowledge, understanding, reasoning.

HOSEA, HOSHEA, OR OSEE—Saviour or safety.

HOSTS—Love, faith, and the knowledge thereof.

HOT—Our God is a consuming fire.

HOUR—State of completeness, continually, perpetually.

HOUSE—Man, the house of God, temple of God, church; full of all good.

HOUSEHOLD—Father-mother-child.

HOUSETOP—Being in God, man's high estate.

HOW—What reason, what cause, what state.

HOWL—Grief because of sin.

HUMAN—The divine nature or bread of life. "Manna," or Egyptian Man-hu.

HUMBLE—To bring back to first principles—to Alpha and Omega.

HUNDRED—Eternal life, full state of perfection, united to God, conjunction.

HUNGER—Force which unfolds me to myself, immortality in its unfolding process, or moving power.

HUNT—To persuade, captivate.

HUR—Truth of doctrine.

HURT—Violate.

HUSBAND—Thy Maker, all that is celestial.

HUSKS—External appearances.

HUTS—Common, general, or particular truths from external.

HUZ—Liberty, whiteness.

HYACINTH—Fire of love and the light of intelligence.

HYMN—Song of praise or joyful recognition.

HYPOCRITE—Devoid of truth, a dissembler.

HYSSOP—Medium of purification.

I

I—One, Jehovah, the unnamed, being in God, ego, impersonal mind.

ICH-A-BOD—No glory, where the glory?

IDDO—Loving, timely, his ornament.

IDEA—Eternal life, Christ, soul.

IDENTITY—That received from God, similitude, like God.

IDLENESS—"Devil's pillow."

IDOL—False religion, falsehood, "nothing at all."

IDOLATERS—Worshipers of self-derived intelligence or traditions of men.

IF—Grant.

IGNORANCE—Commandments of men, or wisdom of men, foolishness.

ILLEGITIMATE—No foundation in truth, doubtful source.

ILLUMINATION—Light of the world, man.

ILLUSIONS—Appearances seen only from appearances, mockery.

ILLUSTRATE—Unfold, show forth, make clear from principle.

IMAGE—Spiritual love, love to the Lord.

IMAGINATION—Ideals formed from idea in mind.

IMLAH—Filled up.

IMMANUEL—God with us. Imma with, nu us, el God.

IMMEDIATELY—Now, here.

IMMERSE—Saturate, with truth, regeneration.

IMMORTAL—Happy, blessed.

IMPIOUS—Those in ignorance of their being.

IMPLANTED—The idea of God.

IMPORTUNITY—Petition, supplication, urgent request.

IMPOSSIBLE (with men)—The food of faith.

IMPOTENT—Dead, natural, carnal.

IMPURITY—Man in himself, from the world's standpoint.

IMPUTE—Lay to one's charge, to suspect.

IN—The soul, center.

INCARNATE—Clothed with the Father's substance.

INCENSE — Prayer, realization, worship, confession of the Lord.

INCLINE—To turn to, to bend.

INCORRUPTIBLE—Eternal, deathless.

INCREASE—Multiply, unfold, growth in grace.

INCREDULOUS—Prejudice to unbelief.

INDEED—Verily, truly.

INDEFINITE—Uncertain.

INDIGENCE—Hunger or the want of good.

INDIGNATION (righteous) — Zeal which swallows its adversary.

INDIVIDUAL—Man in God, indivisible entity.

INEBRIATION—Truth falsified.

INFANCY—Innocence.

INFANT—First degree of love.

INFERIOR—Exterior, that which is in and of itself powerless.

INFIDELITY—Seed of the serpent.

INFINITE—Cause, being, God in man, man in God.

INFIRMITY—Without faith or substance.

INFLAME—Kindling of the spirit.

INFLUX—Pouring in of life, truth, and love.

INFORM—To be intaught, by the inward light.

INGATHERING—Resurrection, awaking to the beauty of holiness.

INGENUITY—Infinite possibilities, God-given, confirmed in man.

INHABIT—To dwell within one's self.

INHERIT—To have and be the life of the Father, to have and be the Lord.

INHERITANCE—God's inheritance is man, man's inheritance is God.

INIQUITY—Witchcraft and sin in general.

INITIATION—Unfolding in the mysteries of the Kingdom of Heaven.

INMOST—Hidden principle of God in man.

INN—Place of protection, rest, and instruction.

INNOCENCE—Essential principle of birth from above.

INSANITY—Chaos, confusion.

INSCRIBE—To be the Book of Life.

INSECTS—Lowest degree of natural affection.
INSPIRATION—Breath of God in man.
INSTINCT—Animal intuition, in-teaching.
INSTRUCTION—Unfolding from the Word.
INSTRUMENTS—Spiritual truths.
INTEGRITY—The good of faith.
INTELLECT—Governing principle of the mind, husbandman, my father.
INTELLIGENCE—Substance, self-existent and eternal mind.
INTEMPERANCE—Fruit of self-love.
INTENTION—The very life of man.
INTERCEDE—To be prepared to receive.
INTERCOURSE—Communion, at-onement.
INTERIOR—Mind and idea.
INTERNAL—Eternal, substance, soul.
INTERPRETATION — Prediction, translation, revelation.
INTESTINES—Last and lowest things.
INTO—Unfoldment, situation, experience.
INTREAT—Use kindly, lead lovingly.

INTRODUCTION—Leading into life.

INTUITION—Interior sight flowing from the Lord or mother.

INVENTOR—The great unfolder of that which is.

INVERSION—Natural state, reversion of truth.

INVISIBLE—God and man (to the world) are unseen and unknown.

INVITED—Drawn by the Father.

INVOKE—The Lord alone invokes or calls out.

INWARD—Invisible.

IRAD—Cain, heresy.

IRE—Corrective action of divine love.

IRON—Strength, power of the word, the truth of faith.

IS, WAS, IS TO COME—Alpha, Omega, the Lord.

ISAAC—Spiritual love, Jah beholds.

ISAIAH—Salvation of the Lord.

ISCARIOT—Man-killer, exterminates.

ISLAND—Truth of faith, those in the truth or the word alone.

ISHMAEL—God that hears, whom God hears.

ISRAEL—Man that sees God.

ISSUE—Offspring.

ITHIEL—Coming of God.

ITSELF—God, being, love, wisdom.

IVAH—Destruction.

IVORY—Natural truth.

J

J—Formerly I; has reference to being.

JAAZANIAH—Whom the Lord will hear.

JABAL—Tent-dweller, doctrine of good things.

JABOC—First insinuation of truth, and dissipation of darkness.

JACINTH—Intelligence from divine love.

JACOB—Word made flesh, external man, or church of the Lord.

JAIR—My light, enlightened.

JAH (Ps. 122-4)—The true and living affirmation of truth.

JAMES (identical with Jacob)—External word.

JAPHETH—Widely spreading, handsome, he that extends or enlarges.

JASHER—The upright or righteous, the book of praises or hymns (the same as Ashir).

JASON—One who receives truth (same as Jesus, or Joshua).

JASPER—White, truth, wisdom.

JAVELIN—Malignant accusation of the adversary.

JAWBONE OF AN ASS—Truth in visible manifestation.

JAWS—External activity, type of will and understanding.

JAZER—He that helps externally.

JEALOUS, ZEALOUS—Divine love in its intensity, watchful.

JEHOASH—Fire of the Lord.

JEBUSITES—Idolatrous beliefs, indifference, sloth.

JEHOIADA—Knowledge of the Lord.

JEHOIAKIM—Appointed of the Lord.

JEHOSHAPHAT—God is judge.

JEHOSHAPHAT VALLEY—Falsification of truth.

JEHOVAH—Old statement of internal man, Jesus Christ, life hid with Christ in God.

JEHOVAH GOD—Mother and father God.

JEHU—Jehovah is He.

JEOPARDY—Truth will swallow all who will not swallow it.

JEREMIAH—Exalted by God.

JERICHO—Instruction in the literal sense.

JEROBOAM—Whose people are many.

JERUSALEM—Mother of us all, holy city.

JESSE—The Lord, wealth, to be, who is.

JESUS—I. Jesus (Rev. 22-16), the Lord in the world, perfect man, affirmation and confirmation of our Father-Mother God, highest idea of God.

JESUS CHRIST—Divine marriage in heaven, of God and man, Father-Son-Holy Spirit visibly manifested.

JETHRO—Excellence of good.

JEWELS—Ornaments of truth, ear-rings, obedience.

JEWS—Lovers of God, and his word made flesh (in the highest sense).

JEWS THAT CRUCIFIED JESUS—Professed lovers who know not the Lord, nor the mysteries of the Kingdom of God.

JEZEBEL—Faith separate from love, worthless doctrine.

JEZREEL—The real church.

JOAB—Who has a second father, worldly man.

JOANNA—Gift of Jehovah, grace of God.

JOB—Natural man, one who speaks from a hollow place.

JOEL—Whose God is Jehovah.

JOHN—Beloved of God.

JOIN—Unite in one, adhere to.

JOHN THE BAPTIST—The Lord as to the Word, preparing the way for Christ, eternal life, doctrine of truth spoken but not embodied.

JONAH—A dove, the Jewish nation, Son of the Eternal. (In the belly of the great fish means "in the heart of the earth.") Sign of Jonah—Christ's death and resurrection.

JONATHAN—Truth of doctrine.

JOPPA—Beauty or comeliness.

JORDAN—Judgment, the land (that which is lowly), the plain (external man), the river (divine truth), passing over the river (introduction to eternal life).

JOSEPH—The Lord (same as Jesus).

JOSEPH SOLD INTO EGYPT—Same as Jesus sold by Judas Iscariot, pure love blessing its enemies.

JOSES—Helped of Jehovah.

JOSHUA—The Saviour.

JOT—A point, the least quantity assignable.

JOURNEY—Order of life in its unfolding.

JOY—Delight of love and truth.

JUBAL—Doctrine of truth.

JUBILEE (the year of)—Fullness of time, the acceptable year of sonship, freedom.

JUDAH (the tribe of)—Praised, he who keeps the first and second commandments.

JUDAS ISCARIOT—Profession of love.

JUDEA—Mind, the church.

JUDGE—Christ.

JUDGMENT—The Word unfolded within itself, the spirit of wisdom and truth in action, determination of God, the Father-Mother confirmed in man.

JUDITH—Praise of the Lord, Jewess.

JUICE—Expression, living witness.

JUST ONE—He who lives by faith, or the substance of things. I, the Lord, the saved in God, hence the Saviour of men.

JUSTICE—Good and truth united in man, giving to man as God gives.

JUSTIFY—To act with God in mind, in word, and thought.

K

K—Borrowed from the Greek.

KEDAR—Blackness, sorrow.

KEEP—To be, to embody.

KEY—Power, knowledge, authority of the King, "I am he that liveth, and have the keys of death and hell."

KICK—Intellectual truth, refusing Christ.

KID—Innocence.

KILL—To take the life of, to deprive man of the truth of his being, or self-evidence.

KIND—Gentle, compassionate, nature of love.

KINDLED—Moved by love, roused by truth.

KINDNESS—Proof of divine love, good will, favor, grace.

KINDRED—Seen in one father-mother.

KINE—Affections of the natural man.

KING—Truth itself. "To this end was I born," ruler.

KINGDOM OF HEAVEN—Atmosphere of the soul, the universal reign of harmony in man, at-one-ment with source.

KISS—Conjunction, union, acknowledgment, confirmation, initiation into the bosom of the Father through the Son.

KISS (of Judas)—Consummate deceitfulness of worldly affection seen and overcome; knowledge of man's divine mission in the world.

KNEE—Adoration, genuine humility.

KNEEL—Willing receptivity.

KNIFE—Truth of faith.

KNOCK—Perpetual presence of the Lord.

KNOT—A binding device.

KNOW—To be, and act upon what I am.

KNOWLEDGE—Substance of the universe with which the earth or man is filled.

KORAH—Damnation.

KUSH—Love and faith.

L

LABAN—Affection of truth, good of a common stock, white, beautiful.

LABOR—Travail, unfoldment, natural man in process of manifesting himself to himself.

LABORERS—All who teach from the Lord.

LACE—Interweaving of truth and life.

LACK—In want, destitution.

LAD—Innocence of youth, infant perception of truth.

LADDER—Man, access to God, lady, Blessed Virgin.

LAKE—Truth in abundance.

LAKE (of fire)—Love of God.

LAMB OF GOD—Embodiment of Father-Mother God, which takes away sin, innocence, the Lord in humanity, meekness, submissiveness, obedience.

LAME—Not walking in faith or the embodiment of Eternal Life.

LAMB SLAIN—Lord unrecognized.

LAMECH—Poor, made low, humble, hence powerful.

LAMENT—Combating evil, true unfolding of good, repentance.

LAMP—Illumination, directive light or guidance, the Word of God, love (Matt. 25-4).

LAND—Man's divine inheritance, the gift of God, holy land, man in God.

LANES—Avenues and ways of men, truths loved and walked in.

LANGUAGE—Means of communication of man with God, measure of man.

LAODICEANS—Faith without the life or works, those who profane truth.

LARGE—Infinite mind, unlimited truth, eternal life.

LASCIVIOUS—Looseness, tendency to wander from wholeness.

LAST—The Lord.

LAST DAY—To-day.

LATCHET—That which fastens or holds.

LATITUDE—Truth.

LATTER DAYS—Now, here.

LAUGHTER—Cheerfulness.

LAVER—Receptive attitude, natural principle.

LAW—Book of Life, or Ten Commandments, Word of God.

LAW AND THE PROPHETS—Faith and the truths of faith.

LAW-GIVER—I, the Lord.

LAWN OR LINEN—Genuine truth.

LAWYERS—(Luke 11-52)—Those who take away the key of knowledge.

LAY—To place, to bring forth, to let be that which is.

LAZARUS—Adam, insensible to love-truth-life, one whom God helps, the dead, or asleep.

LAZULE STONE—Divine sphere, faith embodied.

LEAD TO—Truth leads to truth, unfold, reveal.

LEAD—Evil, falsehood.

LEADER—What is primary in doctrine, Christ.

LEAF—The external fadeless word, ultimates of truth, product, effect.

LEAH—Weary, external worship.

LEAN—Without love.

LEAP—To live unto life.

LEARN—Interiorly, to perceive.

LEAST—The greatest servants of God.

LEATHERN GIRDLE—External word.

LEAVE—To depart from, to give, let be.

LEAVEN—Truth which uplifts, raises.

LEBANON—Spiritual good, incense, white.

LED—Blessedness of truths, revelation.

LEEKS—Corporeal part of man.

LEES—Feast of fat things, truths from good.

LEFT—Remains, that which was in the beginning.

LEGIONS OF ANGELS—Innumerable, unlimited number.

LEGION—Every phase of falsehood.

LEGS—The will and understanding.

LEMUEL—Sacred to God.

LEND—To teach.

LENGTH—Wholeness.

LENTILS—Overshadowing of truth.

LEOPARD—Artful deception of false belief in good and evil.

LEPROSY—Unholiness, universal belief of being born in sin.

LESSER—Truth.

LEST—For fear of.

LET DOWN—An act of submission.

LETTER—Divine word, invisible and visible.

LEVI—Love and mercy, crowned with eternal life.

LEVIATHAN—Scientific in general, self-evidence.

LEWD—Lustful, impure.

LIBERTY—Independence, interior sight, faith in being one spirit.

LICK—Hunger and affection of the unfolding soul.

LIE—To see deception from the vantage ground of truth.

LIE DOWN—Conjunction and consociation, to rest in God.

LIFE—Soul, substance, Christ, God's divine idea, foundation entire, complete, the gift of God, being in God, essential food, man, visible and invisible, I am.

LIFT UP—Finish, to know, to complete, judgment.

LIGHT—Divine truth, delight of love and wisdom, I am, the Lord.

LIGHTNINGS—Instructions of the Lord from within.

LIKE—The same as, in the similitude of, resembling, external appearance.

LIKENESS—Outward form, counterpart, word made flesh.

LILY—New birth, great beauty, love's unfoldment, I am.

LIMIT—The end seen in the beginning, universal law.

LINE—Truth.

LINEN—Truth from God.

LINEN (fine)—Righteousness of saints, quality of the soul.

LINGER—Yield to lower attractions, hesitate between death and life.

LION—Truth in power, affirmation and confession of the Lord.

LIP—Doctrine, internal worship, adoration.

LITTLE ONE—Innocence, obedience to self-evident truth, willingness.

LIVE FOREVER—The Lord Himself.

LIVING—Those who are life eternal.

LIVING SOUL—Man in God.

LIVING WATER—Embodiment of truth.

LO—Behold, being.

LO-AM-MI—Not my people.

LOAVES (five)—Full activities of life in man, the embodied law of God in Christ Jesus.

LOATHE—Aversion.

LOCKS—Radiation of mind.

LOCUSTS—Doctrine without love, ultimate truths spoken without realization.

LODGE—Transient peace, doing to get good, working for reward.

LOFT—Heaven, state of spiritual elevation.

LOFTY—Intellectual pride.

LOGIC—Unfolding of law, effect of self-evidence.

LOINS—Marriage of truth and good, will and understanding.

LO-IS—Better.

LONG FOR—To desire earnestly, to hunger and thirst.

LOOK—To understand.

LOOSE—Set free.

LORD—Supreme ruler, essential good and truth, the one, all in all, Christ our life.

LORD'S PRAYER—The Word of God, I am, the Spirit of the Lord, or the very presence.

LONG-SUFFERING—Embodiment of eternal endurance.

LO-RU-HA-MA—Uncompassionate, without love or mercy.

LOSE—Die to self-consciousness.

LOT—Covered, veiled, the Kingdom of God is the lot of man.

LOT'S WIFE—Falsehood, man's idea of himself.

LOUD VOICE—Voice of thunder, voice of many waters, power of truth; still small voice, soul to soul.

LOVE—Essential bread, essence of God the Father.

LOWLY—Meek.

LOWER THAN HIS ANGELS—Man made, ideal-worshiper.

LUCID—To be wise.

LUCIFER—Self-love, Babel.

LUCIUS—Of light.

LUCRE—Gain, that which perverts judgment of God.

LUD—The knowledge of truth.

LUKE—Light-giver, health-giver.

LUKEWARM—Indifferent, slothful, idle, lawless.

LUMEN—Delusive.

LUMP—All of man, invisible and visible.

LUNGS—Correspond to faith in the understanding.

LUST—Greed, love of separate selfhood and of the world.

LUZ—Separation.

LYDIA—Contention.

LYE—False doctrine.

M

MACEDONIA—Adoration, elevated.

MACHIR—He that knows.

MACROCOSM—Infinite expansion and expansiveness of the wisdom and glory of Being as the Father is.

MAD—Insane, out of truth, chaotic.

MADE—Formed, created.

MAGDALENE—Tower, grand, magnificent.

MAGI—Skilled and taught from within.

MAGICIAN—One who understands the natural tendencies of the carnal mind.

MAGISTRATE—One administering law.

MAGNETISM (animal)—Allurement of the old sense of selfhood, subtle affections of the natural or unregenerate mind.

MAGNIFICENT—Grand, glorious.

MAGNIFY—Expand, unfold, show forth, make visible.

MAGOG—Dissolves, covers, the reign of Gog, external worship.

MA-HA-LA-LEEL—Glory of God.

MAIDS—External serving the internal, affection of the natural.

MAIMED—Unprotected, God-forsaken.

MAJESTY—Glory, power, dignity, grandeur.

MAKE—Cause to be, ordain.

MAKER—The Lord thy God.

MALACHI—One sent.

MALCHUS—King.

MALE CHILD—Child of strength and power.

MALE AND FEMALE—Essential principle of being; (male, the wisdom of love; female, the love of wisdom).

MALEFACTOR—Law-breaker, evil-doer.

MALICE—Hatred.

MAMMON—Riches of the world, knowledge of good and evil.

MAMRE—Fat, elevated, strength, manliness.

MAN—Love and wisdom, the word of God, the highest form of man is woman, eternal life, God's idea of himself, heaven and earth, soul and body.

MAN SERVANT—Natural man as to the truth.

MANASSEH—Forgetting, he that is forgotten.

MANGER—The soul of man, soil, earth, cave, consciousness, place where the animals feed.

MANDRAKES—Marriage of good and truth.

MANIFEST—Unfold, make known, reveal, show forth, display.

MANIFESTATION OF THE LORD—Living presence in man.

MANIFOLD—Many-folded, hidden to the natural mind.

MANNA—Desert bread (hidden wisdom), "man-hu" or human, "What is it?" type of Christ, the real bread.

MANNER—Character, mode of expression.

MANOAH—Rest, house of God.

MANSIONS—States of consciousness, unfolding of love.

MANTLE—External garment, truth of the Word.

MANY—Numerous, numberless.

MARAH—Bitter, quality of.

MARANATHA—The Lord is come.

MARBLE—Sensual principle.

MARCH—The unfolding of truth.

MARCUS—Polite.

MARK—Acknowledgment and confession, knowledge of truth.

MARKET—Acquisition, gain.

MARRED—The vengeance of the Lord, disfigured, deformed.

MARRIAGE—Union of God and man, relationship established in the beginning, in being, principle which is before all things, in which all things consist.

MARROW—Fat things, goodness, substance, hidden idea.

MARS HILL—Supreme council.

MARTHA—Lady, careful.

MARTYR—Confession of the Lord.

MARVELOUS—Omnipotence.

MARY—Blessed Virgin, exalted, queen of the sea, holy woman, wholly divine.

MARVEL—Expansive action of newly perceived wisdom.

MASTER—Leader, Lord, chief, teacher, ruler, truth, one uncontrolled, skilled, conquerer.

MASONS—Master builders.

MASS (holy)—Body of the Lord Jesus Christ.

MATERIAL—Eternal life, faith, important elements or substantial foundation of things.

MATIN—The first dawning of divine understanding.

MATRIX—Opening of the soul to receive the truth, place of receptivity.

MATTER—Mother, earth, soil, what produces.

MATTHEW—Given, gift, eternal life, being in God.

MATURE—Born from above, complete, perfected.

ME—Certainty, self-evidence, the Lord, life, mother.

MEADOW—The word.

MEAL—The truth of faith, manifested word, natural man (the three measures of meal).

MEANS—God the Father-Mother.

MEASURE—To know the quality or inner nature of a thing.

MEASURES AND WEIGHTS—Estimation of things from true judgment.

MEAT—The finished work of God, perfected man, doing the will of God, being as God.

MEDES—Doctrine of the world.

MEDIA AND PERSIA — Faith without works, doing before being, idolatry.

MEDIATOR—Blessed Virgin, perfected man, or love itself.

MEDITATION—Communion, receptivity to the Word.

MEDICINE—The truth of being, counsel or doctrine of the Lord.

MEDIUM—"I am the door," "No man cometh to the Father but by Me."

MEEK—Natural, flowing, yielding, humble, submissive, non-resisting, one who embodies the law of God, blessed.

MEET—To provide, to join.

MEGIDDO—Rich, precious fruit.

MELANCHOLY—Delighting in death and its conditions.

MELCHIZEDEK—King of justice or righteousness.

MELT—Vanish.

MEMBERS—Activities, manifestations of the Lord.

MEMORIAL — Living witness, perpetual presence.

MEMORY—Being, mind, book of life, I am.

MEN—The expansion of man; angels, those in the knowledge and understanding of man.

MEND—Ignorant doctrine; "behold I make all things new."

MENE—To know as to quality, to number.
   TEKEL—To weigh.
   PEREZ—To divide or disperse. (Dan. 5: 25-28.)

MENTION—Communicate.

MERCHANDISE—Exchange of beliefs and opinions, or doctrines, adulteration.

MERCENARY—The good of reward.

MERCHANTS—Those who falsify the Word.

MERCIFUL—Immortal, happy in being righteous.

MERCY—Love itself, I will have mercy because I am it.

MERCY-SEAT—Over-shadowing of God.

MERIBAH—Strife, contention.

MERIT—Virtue, truth, justice, honor, glory of the Lord.

MERRY—Filled with the love of truth.

MESOPOTAMIA—Between, middle.

MESSENGER—Angel, the sent forth, man made, servant.

MESSIAH—Divine truth, the anointed.

MET—Conjunction, atonement.

METALS—Goods and truths of man, the shining of the truths.

METHUSELAH—Man of God, the eighth from Adam.

MICE—Falsities of the sensual, natural loves.

MICAH—Who is as God or Jah.

MICHAEL—Genuine truth.

MICROCOSM—Man, the little world, epitome of the universe.

MIDDAY—Clear light of truth.

MIDDLE—Inmost principle.

MIDIAN—Strife, contention.

MIDNIGHT—Total darkness from falsehood.

MIDST—Principle, inmost, primary, everywhere, in all things.

MIDWIFE—Natural man.

MIGHT—Power of truth.

MIGHTY TO SAVE—The presence of love.

MIGRATE—Rejection.

MILDEW—Non-reception.

MILES—Progression in order of unfoldment.

MILK—First nourishment from the inteacher, truth rooted in faith.

MILK AND HONEY—Truth and the delight of it in good or demonstration.

MILL—Examination and confirmation of truth.

MILLSTONE—Truth serving faith.

MIND—All of man, also all of God, I and my Father, One, the only "I" or "us."

MIND (mortal)—Judgment based on external appearances, carnal mind, Adam.

MINDFUL—Motherly, loving, considerate.

MINERALS—Substance of things organized in animal and vegetable kingdoms.

MINES—Rich source of wealth, Kingdom of Heaven with hid treasure.

MINGLE—Blend, mix.

MINISTER—Servant of truth, unfolder of truth, giver of truth.

MIRACLES—Natural signs following truth embodied.

MIRIAM—The good of faith exalted.

MIRE OF THE STREETS—False doctrine.

MIRROR—Truth.

MIRTH—Joy, delight, gladness.

MIRY CLAY—Flattery of mortal sense.

MISCHIEF—Damage, vexation.

MISERY—Ignorance, darkness.

MISSIONARY—Sent of God, Son of God.

MISTS—Beliefs arising from falsehood and superstition, doctrines of idolatry.

MISTRESS—Affection of interior man.

MITE—Basic principle of truth, the infant Jesus.

MITRE—Intelligence and wisdom.

MIX—Adulterate, profane or falsify truth.

MIZAR—Smallness.

MIZPAH—Watch-tower, one who waits, quality of the Lord's presence.

MIZRAIM—Egypt.

MO—Ma, more.

MOAB—Natural good.

MOAT—Doctrine.

MOB—Disorderly assembly.

MOCK—To deceive, deride, scoff, sneer, scorn, blaspheme.

MOLECH—King.

MOLES AND BATS—Those who seek truth for gain or glory to themselves.

MOLLIFY—To soften or calm.

MOLTEN IMAGE—Formed from human will.

MONEY—Expansion of one, many.

MONTH—A complete state, a new state.

MONUMENT—Resurrection and life.

MOON—Divine idea of man externalized, spiritual good or truth.

MOONLIGHT—Radiation of the Father's presence seen through faith.

MORAL—Reflex of the spiritual, natural and orderly expression of divine law.

MORDECAI—Enlightened, consecrated.

MORE—Great, much expanded.

MORIAH—Chosen by God.

MORNING—Dawn, coming forth, illumination, first and most intense degree of love.

MORNING STAR—I, Jesus, love and wisdom.

MORROW—Revelation of man.

MORTAL—Falsehood, that which has no place in truth.

MORSEL—A trifle, smallest conception.

MORTAR—False appearances, slime, worldly pride.

MORTIFY—Kill through neglect.

MOSES—Law, drawn from the waters, saved out of the waters.
> Mo-she (Egyptian) signifies water child. Mos-heh (Hebrew) signifies one who draws.

MOTE—Falsity.

MOTH—Carnal gaiety, giddiness.

MOTHER—The kingdom of the Lord, New Jerusalem, the church, man's highest unfoldment, Blessed Virgin.

MOUNT—Heaven.

MOUNT OF OLIVES—State of peace.

MOUNT ZION—State of truth.

MOUNTAIN—Love realized, divine good of life.

MOURN—Blessedness, inversion of state.

MOUSE—Sordidly, avaricious.

MOVE—To live, to be, eternal life.

MOUTH—Idea, discourse, doctrine, speech, the word, natural affection, place of least resistance.

MOVED—Act from and with God.

MUCH—Truth.

MUD, OR CLAY—Ultimates in which are truths.

MULE—Affection of truth, obstinacy.

MULTIPLY—To expand in truth.

MULTITUDE—Being unlimited.

MURDER—Denying life.

MURMUR—Complain, state of unbelief.

MUSIC—Harmony of being, life, truth and love.

MUST—Force of principle, truth the all in all.

MUSTARD SEED—Natural man unfolding within himself, the Word, faith expanding into love.

MUTUAL LOVE—That which joins soul and body in one substance.

MYRIAD—Manifold.

MYRRH—That which embalms or preserves.

MYRTLE—Everlasting life, spiritual good.

MYSELF—Self-evident truth.

MYSTERY—Glorified humanity, the word made flesh, the Kingdom of God here and now, me and mine.

MYSTICS—Those initiated into the presence of the Lord.

MYTH—Parable, secret hidden in fable, fanciful narrative covering a great truth, allegory.

N

N—The same as nine, complete.

NAAMAN—Beautiful, agreeable, pleasantness.

NABOTH—The church. Towering.

NADAR—Liberal, prince.

NAHOR—Angry.

NAHUM—Sympathy.

NAIL—Truth supporting beauty, Christ.

NAIN—Beauty.

NAKED—Innocence.

    Head, deprivation of truth or intelligence. Body, deprivation of faith. Loins, deprivation of the good of love.

NAME—Essence of a thing, its nature and quality, reputation of power.

NAME OF THE FATHER—Man in God, the Word was with God.

NAME OF THE LORD—State or quality of faith.

NA-O-MI—Beautiful, full of grace.

NAPH-TALI—Contests, struggle.

NAPKIN—Intelligence of the world.

NARRATE—To perceive.

NARROW—One only, strait.

NATHAN—Gift of God.

NATIONS—Doctrines of the church.

NATURAL GOOD- As in Adam all die (lifted up from the earth), so in Christ all are made alive to life.

NATURAL PRINCIPLE—The spiritual, the immortal.

NATIVITY—Reformation.

NATURE—Ultimate of Creation, recipient of love and wisdom.

NAUGHT—Worthless, nothing, valueless, man separate, apart from God.

NAVEL—Principle of divine motherhood.

NAY—Yea, affirmation of truth.

NAZARETH—Separated, little.

NAZARITE—The Lord, separated unto wholeness.

NEAR—Presence, conjoined by love.

NEBO—Fruitfulness.

NEBUCHADNEZZAR—The great King of Nebo, Prince of the God of this world.

NECESSITY—That which is, lot, irresistible.

NECK—Conjunction between the interior and exterior.

NECKLACE OF GOLD—Highest good realized of spiritual atonement.

NECROMANCER—One who understands the illusion of time.

NEED—Calling to us our own.

NEEDLE (eye of)—Spiritual truth.

NEEDLEWORK—Internal worship.

NEEDY—Destitute, poor.

NEGATIVE—Adam state.

NEHEMIAH—Consolation, rest.

NEIGHBOR—Man collectively.

NER—Lamp, taper.

NERVE OR SINEW—Truth, life, power.

NEST—To dwell, to fulfill, life, mansion, abode, my Father's house.

NETHER MILLSTONE—Man in God, the Holy Mother.

NETHINIMS—Given, consecrated.

NETS—Will and understanding.

NETTLES AND BRAMBLES—Thorns and thistles, rage or burning of self-love.

NEVER—Forever.

NEVERTHELESS—Notwithstanding.

NEW—I am, and its forever unfoldings.

NEW BIRTH—True idea of being, coming forth from one source.

NEW HEAVEN AND NEW EARTH—Eternal life and immortal body, one man, new creature, Father-Mother.

NEW NAME—Acknowledgment of one substance, one faith.

NEW SONG—Confession unto salvation.

NEW TESTAMENT—New statement of being, "I am the resurrection and the life."

NEW WINE—Judgment of God the Father-Mother embodied in My flesh and blood, living witness of the living God.

NEXT—Nearest.

NICHOLAS—Conqueror of the people.

NICODEMUS—Conqueror.

NIGH—Presence.

NIGHT—Obscurity, mother, earth.

NIGHTS (forty)—Combat of self-unfoldment.

NIMROD—Rebel.

NINE—Conjunction, the end of a former state, and the beginning of a new.

NINEVEH—Handsome, agreeable.

NO—The affection of truth.

NOAH—Rest.

NOB—Increase.

NOBLE—True to truth, obedient, faithful.

NOD—Flight.

NOISE (joyful)—Expression or manifestation of life, harmony.

NONE—Not any, which in truth is one complete.

NOON—State of wisdom or full light.

NOPH—Honeycomb.

NORTH—Natural man, innocence.

NOSE OR NOSTRILS—Perception.

NOTHING—From nothing nothing comes, something is all.

NOURISHMENT—Truth from the word of God, "I am the bread of life."

NOW—Presence, being, life eternal, I.

NUMBER—To know the nature and quality of a thing, measure.

NUPTIALS—State of being in Heaven as the Lord.

NUN—Fish.

NURSE—State of innocence.

NURTURE—Nourishment, the bread of life.

NUT—Natural truth.

NYMPHAS—Bridegroom.

O

O—A vowel, used to express a sound corresponding with affection.

OAK—Endurance, quality, strength, firmness, natural man; its leaves, the scientifics and knowledges of truth in him.

OARS—That by which the understanding speaks.

OATH—Confirmation, self-evidence, I am, the Oath of God, the end of strife.

OB—To thrust in, or in front.

OBADIAH—Servant of Jah or the Lord.

OBDURATE—Hard-hearted, stiff-necked.

OBED—Worshiper.

OBED-EDOM—Red, earthy man.

OBEDIENCE—To hear, and yield to.

OBEISANCE—State of reverence, submission, humility.

OBLATION—Worship, true offering, by bearing or bringing the Lord's body.

OBSCURITY—Internal man, invisible substance, soul, Son in the bosom of the Father.

OBSERVE—That which is kept in being.

OBTAIN—To hold.

OCCASION—Lot, fate, destiny.

OCCULT—Hidden, secret.

OCCUPY—Resting within the veil, faith unto salvation.

OCEAN—The great deep, abyss, Infinite mind, source, mother.

ODOR—Fragrance, perfume, affection of faith and love, perception of peace.

OF—Begotten, in, manifest.

OFFENSE—Cause of stumbling, opinions and beliefs of the world.

OFFERINGS—Worship, first fruits.

OFFICERS—Those who execute the law.

OFFICE—Charge of trust, Kingdom of Heaven.

OFFSPRING—Those principled in being in God, embodying eternal life.

OFTEN OR OFT—Endless unfoldment.

OG—Giant, evils of every kind.

OIL—Good of love, prayer, knowledge ultimated in itself, consecration, to kindle, regeneration.

OINTMENT—Unction, that which sanctifies, that which prepares for the true lifting up.

OLD—Presence of the new state, honorable.

OLD AGE—The last time.

OLD MEN AND WOMEN—Confirmed truths.

OLD TESTAMENT—Mystery of being, faith, heaven.

OLIVE—Truth of holiness, beauty of wholeness, holy one.

OLIVE TREES—Soul and body, two witnesses.

OLIVE LEAF—Truth of faith.

OLIVET—Place of olives, divine love.

OLYMPAS—Victory.

OMEGA—The Lord, man in God.

OMER—Sufficient quantity.

OMIT—Neglect.

OMNIPOTENCE—All potent, all power.

OMNIPRESENCE — Presence unbounded and universal.

OMNISCIENCE—Knowing all things at once and in all ways.

OMRI—Sheaf, my portion is the Lord, Jah.

ON—Near or at.

ONAN—Trespass, iniquity.

ONCE—Perpetual truth of being.

ONE—Being, all, man in God, heaven and earth.

ONESIMUS—Usefulness or serviceable.

ONIONS AND GARLIC—Lowest natural, or sensual.

ONLY BEGOTTEN—All that proceeds from God, gotten of God alone.

ONYX OR BDELLIUM—Myrrh, perfume used for embalming.

OPEN—Communicate, unclose, conjoin.

OPERATE—Regenerate.

OPERATION—Progression of life in its unfolding.

OPHEL—Tower, elevation, a hill.

OPHIR—Plenty.

OPINION—Supposition, to suspect.

OPPRESS—Overpower, overburden.

OPULENCE—Knowledge.

ORACLE—Mouthpiece or living witness of God, man.

ORDAIN—Appoint, set, choose, determine by lot.

ORDER—The Lord, Heaven's first law, being life.

ORDINANCE—The Word of God.

ORGAN—Spiritual good, harmony.

ORGANIZE—Arrange from divine law.

ORIGIN—Source, first cause, Father-Mother, beginning.

ORIGINAL SIN—Mortal mind, nothingness of nothing. Man's idea of himself, separate from God.

ORION—The giant.

ORNAMENT—Holy truth, divine in externals.

ORNAN—Slender, lank.

ORPHANS—Innocence, natural man.

OTHERS—The within man.

OTHNIEL—Lion of God.

OUGHT—Held, bound.

OURS—All things, divine inheritance.

OUT—Within.

OUTCAST—Rejected, in darkness.

OUTER DARKNESS—Falsehood.

OUTER AND INNER—Soul and body, one only.

OUTSIDE—Unredeemed, separate.

OVEN—Love of God.

OVER—Within.

OVERFLOW—To expand, multiply, increase from within.

OVERCOME—To receive and embody.

OVERLOOK—Dominant state, understanding.

OVERSHADOW—Christ's presence, the one thing needful.

OVERTAKE—Communicate.

OVERTURN—Punish.

OVUM—Man, seed.

OWE—Possess naturally, to hold in being.

OWL—Falsification of truth, world's wisdom.

OWN—Inherent, recognized of the Father.

OX—Natural state.

OXEN (five yoke)—Natural affections.

OZIAS—Strength from the Lord.

P

P—The masculine article in the Coptic language.

PADAN-ARAM—Of a pair or of two.

PAGAN—Idolatrous, heathen, form worshiper, darkness.

PAIN—Agitation, purification.

PAINT—Hypocrisy, sanctimony.

PAIRS—Things that correspond, truth and good, soul and body.

PALACE—The consciousness of being in God, state of will and understanding conjoined to the Lord.

PALE HORSE—Signifies lack of life or vitality, no knowledge of truth.

PALESTINA—Wanderer.

PALMS—Victory, confession of the Lord, holy festivity in the love of truth.

PALM TREES—Rest and pleasantness in the realization of truth.

PALMER WORM—False belief, wandering, opinion.

PALSY—Fearful, unbelieving.

PAMPHYLIA—Of every tribe, all.

PAN—Doctrine, adulterated.

PAPACY—Authority vested in one.

PAPER—Scroll, book.

PAPS—Spiritual love.

PARABLES—To place in pairs, or set together one thing with another.

PARACLETE—Divine truth, one called of God, comforter.

PARADISE OF GOD—Truth of wisdom and faith, heaven.

PARALLEL—Communication or atonement between soul and body.

PARALYTIC—Faithless, fearful.

PARAN—State of illumination, beauty, glory.

PARCHED—Love of self and the love of the world.

PARDON—Forgiveness, give back, remit.

PARENTS—Source, beginning, God the Father-Mother.

PARROT—Imitator, one who repeats what he hears.

PART—The whole, three in one.

PARTAKER—Sharer, or one of the same nature.

PARTICULAR—Pertaining to one.

PARTRIDGE—One who brings forth from externals.

PASCHAL LAMB—Innocence, type of unity, the Lord's own sacrifice, peace offering, thank offering, type of the Covenant.

PASCHAL SUPPER—Communion and conjunction with the Lord.

PASHUR—Extension, expansion.

PASS—To flow in, inhabit.

PASSAGE—Free reception.

PASS AWAY—Resurrection.

PASS THE NIGHT—Judge from truth.

PASSOVER—The glorification of man, putting on righteousness, incorruption.

PASSION—Love of truth to the degree of putting all enemies under one's feet.

PASTOR—Shepherd, Teacher, Master, the Lord Himself.

PASTURE—Spiritual nutrition.

PATH—The way, the truth, the life.

PATHROS—Mouth full of dew.

PATIENCE—Substance, same as faith.

PATMOS—Illumination, separated unto God.

PATRIARCH—Head of a family.

PATRIOTISM—Love of the Kingdom of God, the true and only Fatherland.

PATTERN—Example, after the image of the Father.

PAUL—Little, small; (Heb.) Saul, demanded or asked for.

PAUPER—Worshiper of externals, a vacuum.

PAVILION OR TENT—The dwelling of the Lord.

PAY—To render that which is due.

PEACE—Union of God and man, divine salutation.

PEACOCK—Pride of external worship.

PEARLS—Acknowledgment of the Lord in all ways.

PECULIAR PEOPLE—Those who keep the Word by being it.

PEKAH—Vision of God, at liberty.

PELEG—Division.

PELICAN—Affection of the false.

PELLUCID—Filled with light.

PEN—Finger of God, the Holy Spirit.

PENIEL—Vision of God.

PENNY—All, the whole, unit of divine measurement.

PENTECOST—Fiftieth.

PEOPLE—Doctrine, interior truths.

PERCEIVE—Accepting the operations of God in man, seeing with the Father or by faith.

PERCEPTION—Essence of sight, internal speech, or being.

PERDITION—State of the beast or ungodly.

PERENNIAL—Age-abiding, regenerate.

PERFECT MAN—The Lord alone.

PERFECTION—Being ultimated in the living.

PERFORM—Execute, fulfill.

PERFUME—Sweetness of truth and love.

PERGAMOS—Height, elevation, good works.

PERIL—Uncertainty, of little faith.

PERIOD—Fullness of time, state of affection.

PERISH—State of unbelief, nothingness.

PERIZZITE—Wrath, dwelling in villages, or belief of separation.

PERJURY—Denying the truth of being as the Father is.

PERMANENCE—Truth of being in God.

PERMISSION—Divine law of liberty.

PERPETUAL—Everlasting, eternal.

PERPLEXED—Memory of the world, or of exteriors.

PERSECUTE—Inflict with temptation, to harass.

PERSEVERE—Salvation from within out, constant unfolding of me to myself.

PERSIA—Land of horses, nail.

PERSON—That which appertains to man.

PERSUASION — Infatuation, suffocation, that which carries away the use of reason, deprives of freedom.

PERVERSE—Stubborn in error.

PERVERT—To change.

PESTILENCE—Vastation of good, visitation of evil.

PETER—Primary principle of the church, truth without the embodiment of faith.

PETITION—Prayer, confession of faith.

PHARAOH—Natural man, scientifics. The sun.

PHAREZ—Son of Judah, breaking forth violently.

PHARISEES—Form-worshipers, hypocrites.

PHARPAR—Fruit-producer, the rapid, nimbleness.

PHE-BE—Pure, shining.

PHE-NI-CE—Red, purple, land of palms.

PHILADELPHIA—Love of man from the Lord, brotherly love.

PHILIP—Lover of horses, warlike.

PHILISTINES—Those who conceive false principles and reason from them.

PHILOLOGUS—Lover of words or of learning.

PHINEAS—Love and the things which are of love. Mouth of brass, brazen mouth.

PHLEGON—Burning with zeal.

PHUT—Knowledge from the literal sense.

PHYLACTERIES—Good in external form, having relation to action.

PHYSICIAN—Preservation from sin, the Lord.

PICTURES—Images of mind, doctrines.

PIECES—Dissipation of falsehood.

PIERCE—Destruction of the Word, crucifixion.

PIETY—The good of love.

PIGEON—Innocence.

PILATE—Armed with a dart.

PILGRIM—In the wilderness, under the law.

PILLAR—Supporting principle.

PILLAR OF CLOUD AND OF FIRE—The Lord.

PILLOWS—Things which are under the head, communications with the inmost.

PILOTS—Those in wisdom from the Word.

PINNACLE—Of high understanding.

PIPERS—Those in divine love.

PIPES—Joys of the love of truth.

PISGAH—Piece, fortress, peak, part.

PISON—Extension of the mouth, intelligence of faith. Intellect, outpouring.

PIT—State of temptation.

PITCH—Covetousness.

PITCH A TENT—Measure or fix a habitation, conjunction.

PITCHER—Man in receptive state.

PITY—Divine compassion.

PLACE—State of consciousness.

PLAGUES—Evils of self-love.

PLAIN—All of doctrines, ultimates of the church.

PLANETS—Unfoldings of truth from within.

PLANKS—Supports from truth.

PLANT—Regenerate.

PLATE OF GOLD—Illustration of love from the Lord.

PLATTER—State of consciousness.

PLAY—Action of mind, affection of truth.

PLEAD—Intercede, set right in judgment.

PLEASANT—Delight in wisdom.

PLEASURE—Satisfaction in the knowledge of the Lord.

PLEDGE—Reception of truth.

PLEI-A-DES—Stars of the sailors.

PLOUGH—To implant truth in good.

PLOUGHSHARES—The good set forth or perfected in truth.

PLUMMET, OR PLUMBLINE—Measure of truth which destroys evil.

POISON—Hypocrisy, deceit, falsehood.

POLISHED—The radiance of faith.

POLLUTION—The truth of faith defiled.

POLYTHEISM—Plurality of gods.

POMEGRANATES—Doctrines from the natural man.

POMP—Vain-glory.

PONDER—Study, concentrate, wisdom embodied.

POOLS—Intelligence.

POOR—Uninstructed, destitute.

POPLAR TREE—Same as oak—strength.

PORCH—Outward things which cohere with the interior.

PORT, OR HAVEN—Conclusion of truth, rest.

PORTICO—Externals of the mind.

PORTION OR INHERITANCE—Heaven and earth, union with God through the Lord, soul and body.

POSSESS—To be.

POSSESSIONS—Spiritual riches.

POSSIBLE—That which is.

POSTERIOR—Exterior.

POSTERITY—Generation.

POSTPONE—Stifle, reject, kill.

POSTS OF THE DOORS—Natural truths.

POT—Doctrine.

POTENT—Powerful, truth.

POTIPHAR—Scientifics.

POTTAGE—Heap of doctrines.

POTTER—Regeneration, reformation.

POTTER'S VESSEL—Self-derived intelligence.

POUND—Good from the Word.

POUR OUT—Influx of truth from the Lord.

POVERTY—Destitution.

POWDER—Love of self.

POWER—Jehovah, man in God, Christ Jesus.

PRAISE—Worship.

PRAY—To unfold through love.

PRAYER—Speaking with God, communication, realization of being.

PRAYER (the Lord's)—Ultimating the principle of life, love and truth, self-unfoldment, making the invisible substance visible.

PRAYING—Demonstrating or manifesting the truth of one's self.

PREACH—Discourse upon being, proclaim the acceptable year, pronounce the truth of the Kingdom of God.

PRECEPTS—Internals of the Word.

PRECIOUS STONES—Spiritual intelligence.

PRECIOUS THINGS—Spiritual things.

PREDESTINATE—That which is in the eternal substance before manifestation, fore-appointment of events.

PREDICTIONS—Prophesies, that which relates to being.

PREPARE—Introduce, open the way, to make ready.

PRESENCE—Face, acknowledgment of the Lord.

PRESENT—A gift, reward, recompense.

PRESENT TIME—Now, including past and future.

PRESERVATION—Perpetual creation.

PRESS—The truth of faith.

PREVAIL—Overcome, to have power, predominate, succeed.

PREVENT—Hinder, go before, pre-occupy.

PREY—To spoil, plunder, that which is seized.

PRICE—Ransom, salvation of man, at-one-ment with God, redemption.

PRICKS—Holy Spirit and its operations in man.

PRIDE—The love of self, loftiness.

PRIEST—The Lord Himself.

PRIESTS AND ELDERS—Those who claim to teach truth.

PRIMARY—First, Father-Mother, source, seed.

PRIMITIVE—The beginning.

PRINCE—Power of the Lord.

PRINCE OF PEACE—Christ.

PRINCE OF THIS WORLD—Man mortal, carnal, material.

PRINCIPAL—Love and wisdom, Kingdom of God.

PRINCIPLES—Basic statements of being.

PRISCILLA—Woman, ancient.

PRISON HOUSE—State of falsehood and superstition.

PRISONERS—Captives.

PRIVATELY—Secretly, individually, separately, personally.

PRIZE—Reward, recompense.

PROCEED—To go forth, to make manifest.

PROCESS—Working of eternal life from within out.

PROCLAIM—To utter openly, to set forth in truth.

PROCURE—Externalize, effect.

PRODIGAL SON—One who misapplies his riches, or sets aside the truth of his being for falsehood.

PRODIGY—Confirmation of divine truth.

PRODUCE—To bring forth, to yield from faith and love.

PROFANE—Deny being, depart from truth, reject eternal life.

PROFIT—Benefit, advantage.

PROGRESS—Expand from cause to effect.

PROLONG—Extend.

PROPHET—The Lord, the only true prophet.

PROMISE OF GOD—Jesus Christ.

PROOF—Word made flesh, man the proof of God.

PROPITIATION—Operation of love.

PROSELYTE—Newcomer by persuasion.

PROSPER—Thrive, understand, know, and obey.

PROSTITUTE—Doubt or deny purity any where.

PROSTRATE—Attitude of humility.

PROTECT—Defend.

PROUD—Those in self-love, or beliefs of the world, rich in man-made conjectures or suppositions.

PROVE—To try, to establish through faith, to demonstrate from self-evidence.

PROVENDER—The good of scientifics.

PROVERB—Parable, word, logos, statement.

PROVIDE—See before, furnish, place at hand.

PROVIDENCE—Divine love in operation in man.

PROVINCE—State of consciousness.

PROVISION—Multiplication of truth.

PROVOKE—Trouble, agitate, call into action, excite, to rouse.

PRUDENCE—Comes from God.

PRUDENTLY—Acting from the Lord.

PRUNE—To prepare for reception.

PRUNING-HOOKS — Truths of doctrine founded in wisdom, knowledge of being.

PSALMS—Harmonious discourse of life.

PSALTERIES—Spiritual good, confessions of truth.

PUBLICANS—Gentiles who received the Lord, man of the world.

PUBLISH—Magnify, proclaim.

PUBLIUS—Common.

PUDENS—Modest.

PUL—External worship. Strong, powerful.

PULSE—Seeds, divine truth in doctrine of the Word.

PURCHASE—Make room for, to obtain, acquire.

PUNISHMENT—Consummation of evil.

PURE—Genuine, unadulterated, those in the good of divine love.

PURGATORY—Hades, death of carnal desire.

PURGE—Cast out, clarify, cleanse.

PURPLE—Genuine good, royalty, blending of love and wisdom, flame of fire.

PURSE AND SCRIP—Knowledge of truth or the Kingdom of Heaven.

PURSUE—To cause to disappear, to drive out, expel.

PUSH—To expand, force by truth.

PUT—To place, order, or apply.

Q

QUAIL—Delight, bird of the sea, natural principle.

QUAKE—Waving of or moving of the Spirit upon the face of the waters.

QUAKER—Those instructed by influx from the Spirit, or the inward light.

QUALITY—State of expansion.

QUANTITY—Predicated of truth.

QUARREL—Belief of separation, or dispute.

QUARTERS—Kingdom of God.

QUEEN—The church as a wife.

QUEEN OF SHEBA—Wisdom and intelligence of the Son of man, the oath of God, repose.

QUENCH—Extinguish, put out, repress.

QUESTION—To lay open, unfold, expand.

QUICK—The living word.

QUICKEN—Bring to life, raise the dead.

QUICKLY—Certain, full.

QUICKSAND—Falsehood, tradition, worldly opinion.

QUIESCENCE—Resting silent, having no sound.

QUIETNESS—State of peace, tranquility.

QUILLS (or feathers)—Spiritual good.

QUINTATE—To take a fifth.

QUITE—Totally, perfectly, entirely.

QUIVER—The Word.

R

RA—Again, the same as Re.

RAAMAH—Greatness, thunder, company.

RAAMSES—Worldly wanderings, king of this world and his unfoldings.

RABBATH—Falsification of truth.

RABBI AND TEACHER—The doctrine of truth.

RACA—Vile, to account as nothing.

RACE—Journey from seed to seed.

RACHEL—Affection of interior truth.

RADIATION—The light of heaven, the Lord's love.

RAGE—Fallen from grace, self-centered.

RAGS—Righteousness of the world's beliefs, doctrines founded upon man-made theories.

RAIMENT—Genuine truth.

RAINBOW—Equality of divine truth, sign of the covenant, conjunction, or at-one-ment.

RAIN—Blessing, downpouring of the water of life.

RAISED—Realization of truth, consciousness of being eternal life.

RAM—Natural man, as to the good of charity, elevated.

RAMAH—Sublime, natural or ultimate principle, height.

RAMPART—Doctrinals.

RAN—Spiritual development or expansion of man in God.

RANKS—Planes, correlative powers.

RANSOM—Purification by truth.

RAPHAEL—Ministry in heaven.

RAT—Sordidly avaricious.

RATHER—More properly, or readily, in a greater degree.

RATIO—Equality, degree.

RATIONAL—From the principle of good.

RAVEN—Falsities, den of thieves.

RAW—Without the good of love.

RAZOR—The keenness of truth.

REACH—To shut out.

READ—To perceive, understand and embody or form.

READY—Prepared, in a state of receptivity, willingness.

REAP—To execute judgment, sower and reaper are one, reception of truth.

REASON—Compare cause with effect, discriminate.

REBECCA—Fetter, cord, affection.

REBEL—State of servitude.

REBUKE—Purify, cleanse.

RECEIVE—Acknowledge, confess.

RECEPTACLE—Will and understanding in man.

RECKON—Render decision, judge.

RECOGNITION—Confession, seeing as the Father sees.

RECOLLECT—To remember, to resurrect.

RECOMPENSE—Reward, being in God.

RECORD—Trinity in unity, the gift of God, Father-Mother-Son.

RECONCILED—Satisfied, at rest.

RED—Power of love, strength of love, name, Edom, Eden, Adam.

RED SEA—Perception of love.

REDEEM—Vindicate, set free, liberate.

REDEEMER—Jehovah, the Lord.

REDEMPTION—Ransom, through the gift of God.

REDUCE—To begin at the beginning, regenerate.

REED—Natural man, feeble power.

REED LIKE UNTO A ROD—Power through self-evidence, "golden rod," knowledge of truth and love.

REED SHAKEN WITH THE WIND—Doctrine not found in truth.

REFINE—Restore, prove and reprove by principle.

REFLECT—Ponder, to throw light, to give attention.

REFORMATION—Restoration by the Lord's presence.

REFRAIN—To abstain, hold back.

REFRESH—Invigorate, revive.

REFUGE—Protection in truth, man in the stronghold of faith.

REFUSE—Deny, reject.

REGARD—Consider, esteem.

REGENERATION—New birth by grace and truth.

REGION (round about)—Relative thought.

REHOBOAM—Enlarger of the people.

REHUM—Compassionate.

REIGN—Rule in power, or have dominion in the Lord.

REINS—Quantity and quality of truths, searching the within and without.

REJECT—Cast off.

REJOICE—Radiance of the good of love and truth.

RELATION TO GOD—At-one-ment with source in soul and body.

RELEASE—To set free, give true sonship.

RELIEVE—Bring into the light of truth.

RELIGION—Love, which unites or binds back to the substance of things.

REMAIN—State of being eternal life, seed of God, abiding in Me.

REMALIAH—Ornament of God.

REMEMBER—To keep in mind, to find being in God, to bear in consciousness the truth of what I am, conjunction.

REMISSION OF SIN—Giving up of sin, true repentance.

REMNANT—That which remains, the soul and body.

REMOVE—Change state of belief.

REMUNERATION—Mutual love.

REND—To be without faith.

RENDER—Restore, give back or forgive.

RENEW—Unfold, expand in truth.

RENOWN—Much thought of, commanding attention.

REPAY—Compensate.

REPAIR—To see and be that which is, to raise up in truth.

REPENTANCE—To look at the substance of being, embody the Lord Himself.

REPLENISH—Regenerate, endless unfoldment.

REPORT—The witness of truth.

REPROACH—The world's edict of man, falsehood claiming for itself truth.

REPROVE—Bring forth light in darkness, or truth in place of error, true judgment.

REQUEST—Prayer is self-unfoldment, realization of being.

REQUIRE—Demand, call forth, state of affirmation.

RESEMBLE—Unity, likeness.

RESIDUE—The Lord and His people.

RESIN—Myrrh, used for embalming, truth founded in self-evidence.

RESIST—Oppose, man cannot of himself resist evil.

RESPECT — Consideration, acceptance, honor.

RESPIRATION—Life and its action.

RESPOND—To know, and be.

REST—Being in God, man at-one with his source.

RESTITUTION—Fulfillment of the law and the prophets.

RESTORATION—I and my Father are one.

RESURRECTION—To come to life, light and salvation, not as an observer, but in being it.

RETURN—To be that which is, state of conscious being immortal.

REUBEN—God's mercy, vision of the Son.

REVELATION—Unfoldment in truth from perception, or by the living voice.

REVENGE—Self-love, disease, also judgment of truth.

REVERENCE—Acknowledgment and confession of the Lord.

REVILE—Accusation based on a false assumption.

REVIVAL—Restoring to the recognition of the Father's presence.

REWARD—Conjunction, union with God.

REZIN—Firm, strong, good will.

RHYTHM—Speech of love.

RIB—Substance of man, bone of the breast, vital or essential inherency, wisdom.

RIBBAND OF BLUE—Faith interwoven with love, loyalty to law.

RICH MAN—One who embodies the Word of God.

RIDDLE—Parable, proverb.

RIDE—State of progress, expansion from perfection to perfection.

RIGHT—What is predicated of truth and good.

RIGHT HAND—South, one in faith, or in power, Son in the bosom of the Father, uncreate man.

LEFT HAND—According to the direction of the Lord, north.

RIGHTEOUSNESS—True judgment, light of the world, according to the divine law.

RIMMON—Exalted.

RING—Confirmation of power, eternal life, conjunction, marriage.

RIPE—Complete, full, finished within and without, soul and body.

RISE—Be truth itself, come forth as I am.

RISEN—Predicated of the living God.

RIVER—Influx of life from the Father, the flowing of wisdom from God to man.

ROAD—Mental proceeding, between cause and effect.

ROAR—The voice of truth filling the whole earth.

ROAST—Saved by fire.

ROBBERS—Belief of being less than life, those who try to climb up without knowing they are already whole.

ROCK—The Lord as to the truth of the Word.

ROD OR STAFF—Rod is knowledge; staff is demonstration, soul and body.

ROLL (away the stone)—Removal of falsehood, uncovering the truth.

ROLLS—Books of divine truth, the Word of God.

ROME—Strength, power.

ROOF—Inmost, head.

ROOM—State of consciousness.

ROOT—Love, invisible substance.

ROPE OR CORD—Conjunction.

ROSE—Delight of truth and wisdom. I delight in the law of the Lord.

ROTTEN—Unprincipled, unsubstantial.

ROUGH PLACES—Falsities of ignorance.

ROUND ABOUT—The Lord, omnipresence.

ROWERS—Intelligence, doing.

ROYAL—That which pertains to the Kingdom of Heaven.

RUBY—Celestial flame of love.

RUDDY—Whiteness of truth.

RUFUS—Red.

RUHAMAH—Having obtained mercy, compassionate.

RULE—Record in Heaven, trinity in unity; three is the rule—Father-Mother-Son.

RUIN—The judgment.

RUMORS—Discussions and strifes.

RUN—Agreement.

RUSHES—Knowledges from the sensual plane.

RUST—Indolence, disuse.

RUTH—Friend, satisfied.

RYE—Interior truth.

S

S—Denotes seven.

SABBATH—Rest, conjunction with the Lord, covenant sign of at-one-ment.

SACK—Receptacle, natural principle.

SACKCLOTH — Lamentation, distress, mourning, ignorance.

SACRAMENT—Sacred union of God and man, oath.

SACRIFICE—Glorification of the Lord's humanity, true offering of soul and body unto the living God.

SAD—Ignorant, blind.

SADDLE—Prepare.

SADDUCEES—Those who say there is no resurrection, darkness of unbelief.

SAFE—Lose in the Lord.

SAID (the Lord)—Action of God, revelation, confirmation.

SAILORS—Those who trust in the truth.

SAINTS—Holy, perfect, pure, wise from the standpoint of God's wisdom.

SAKE—Purpose, end.

SALATHIEL—Loan of God, I have asked of God.

SALEM—Tranquility, peace, complete.

SALMON—Peaceable, perfect.

SALT—I am life, truth, love, knowledge from God.

SALUTE—Acknowledge, confess, honor that which is.

SALVATION—Presence of truth, the unfoldment of life.

SAMARIA—Pertaining to a watch, his guard, his prison, his throne.

SAMSON—Like the sun, same as the Son of God, sun man.

SAMUEL—Name of God, placed of God.

SANCTIFY—Save in truth, or in the Word of God.

SANCTUARY—Soul and body, habitation of God.

SAND—Spiritual truths, hidden infinite possibilities in man.

SANG—Harmony in the soul's demonstration of itself.

SANHEDRIN—The council, the seventy, the grand man.

SAPPHIRE—Beautiful.

SAPPHIRE STONE—Faith, quality of the Word spoken from God.

SARAH—Princess, Lady, Holy Mother, Virgin.

SARAI—Contentious.

SARDIS—Song of joy.

SAT—Fixed in truth, at rest in self-evidence.

SATAN—I am mortal, material, corrupt, unholy, totally depraved in nature.

SATISFIED—Filled with love, life and truth, immortal in soul and body.

SAUL—Soul, soil, asked for, demanded.

SAVED—To be taught of God.

SAVIOUR—The gift of God, the Lord our life.

SAW—Eyes opened to truth.

SAY—To know, and speak from knowledge, instruct.

SAYING—Proverb, words of truth.

SCALES—Fallacies of sense.

SCARLET—Truth of the Word in the letter, fire of love.

SCATTERED—Separation, dissipation.

SCENT—Perception.

SCEPTRE—Truth in power and government.

SCEVA—Prepared.

SCHOOL—Rest in concentration, freedom in truth.

SCORCH—Touched with self-love.

SCORNFUL—One who ignores truth, life, love.

SCORPION—Deadly persuasion.

SCOURGED—Perverted, mocked.

SCRIBE—Worldly wisdom, adulteration.

SCRIP—Knowledge of good from observation.

SCRIPTURE—Sacred word, man in God, word in the beginning.

SCROLL—Written word.

SEA—Truth in its termination and collection, natural man.

SEAL—To distinguish as finished and complete, conclude.

SEAL OF THE LIVING GOD—To know that I am life.

SEAMLESS—Without separation, indivisible.

SEARCH—To see and know by revelation.

SEASONS—States of unfoldment.

SEAT—Judgment of truth.

SECT—Belief of separation.

SECOND COMING OF THE LORD—Realization of being life itself, the Blessed Virgin Mother.

SECOND DEATH—Leaving beliefs and opinions, rising to life, dying in the Lord.

SECRET—Presence of the Lord, bosom of the Father.

SECURITY—Rest in the truth.

SEDUCE—To lead away.

SEE (formerly she)—Intuition, affection of understanding.

SEED—Man is the seed of God, substance.

SEED TIME—Knowledge of being, acceptance of truth.

SEEING—Is being, acknowledgment, confession of faith.

SEEK—To unfold by love of the Father.

SEEN—Being the same yesterday, to-day and forever, the perfect use of the faculties of man.

SEER—In the spirit of the Lord.

SEIR—Hairy, goat, ragged.

SE-LAH—Denotes harmony, that which unites, musical direction, that which pertains to science. Silence.

SELF—Belief of man, separate and apart from God, nothing but falsehood.

SELF-EVIDENCE—Eternal life which comes without argument, the gift of God.

SELL—Teach doctrine, to give, bind tares into bundles and burn them, and gather wheat into my barn.

SEND—Reveal.

SENSATION—That which is derived from love and wisdom.

SENSES—Principal activities of man, that inherency of man called "seas," sheep of my fold.

SENT OF GOD—Man the living witness of God, teacher from God.

SEPARATION—In the highest sense, the acknowledgment of at-one-ment.

SEPULCHRE—Life or heaven.

SERAIAH—Prince of the Lord.

SERAPHIM—Fiery or burning ones.

SERPENT—Man, wisdom of God, symbol of the sun.

SERVANT—One who keeps, or holds; man keeps the gift of God by being it.

SET—Fixed, appointed.

SETH—Appointed, placed, sprout.

SEVEN—Completeness, rest in being, holy number.

SHADOW—Suggestion.

SHADRACH—Soft, tender, friend.

SHAKE—Acknowledgment that I am moved by the Holy Spirit, to liberate, set free.

SHALLUM—Peaceable, perfect recompense.

SHAME—Confusion, discord, disease.

SHAPHAT—A judge.

SHARON—His song, a plain.

SHARP—Predicated of truth, accurate.

SHAVE—To make clean.

SHEAF—Doctrine of Him that sent me.

SHEAR—To cut away.

SHEBA—An oath, or league.

SHECHEM—Shoulder, ridge, early in the morning.

SHEEP—External flock, means activities of mind found in the body, senses.

SHEEPFOLD—Substance of things, heaven.

SHEKEL—Price of truth and good.

SHEM—Name, fame, renown.

SHEMIAH—Heard of God, that which obeys God.

SHEPHERD—I, life, the Lord.

SHEW—Instruct, reveal, unfold.

SHEW-BREAD—The Lord, when an hungered as David, we eat.

SHIELD—Defense of truth, life, love.

SHILOH—Resting place, abundance, sent.

SHIMEI—Renowned.

SHINAR—Lion, land, the watch of him that sleeps.

SHIP—State of unfoldment or consciousness, knowledge of truth and good, creation of truth, from the word shape.

SHINE—That which is pure, exempt from falsity.

SHITTIM—Turns away, a gum (substance imperishable).

SHOE—That which clothes the understanding.

SHOOK—Awakened, moved by truth.

SHOOT—To deceive.

SHORE—Where land and water meet, or where soul and body meet.

SHORT—Quickly, speedily, truth cutting off error.

SHOULDER—All power.

SHOUT—Worship from the good of love.

SHOWERS—Refreshing influx of truth.

SHRUB—Expansion of truth in lesser degree than tree.

SHULAMITE—Peaceful.

SICKLE—That which puts an end to falsehood, divine truth of being.

SICKNESS—Belief of hatred, the unfoldment of sin.

SHUT—That which is finished by God.

SIDE—Spiritual unfoldment, interior principle; (right side) at one with God, drawn out from God.

SIDON—Fishing, hunting.

SIEGE—To straiten with truth.

SIFT—Teach, instruct.

SIGHT—Unfoldment of the light of truth, understanding.

SIGN—Token of union with the Father is man, the only sign given.

SIGN OF JONAH—Death and resurrection is signified, which is man as he is in truth.

SIGNET—Confirmation, signifies finished work.

SIHON—One who smites.

SILAS—The third.

SILENCE—Tranquility of faith.

SILK—Truth resplendent.

SILOAM—Sent.

SILVANUS—Forest or woods.

SILVER—Scientific truth, intellectual reasoning, rational truth, words of the Lord.

SIMEON—One heard, hears and obeys.

SIMPLE—Self-evident, the law of being, the yoke of Christ.

SIN—Denying the truth of being life, to depart from God, love of self separate.

SIN—Clay.

SINAI—Heaven, the Lord.

SINCERE—Pure, unmixed, genuine.

SINEWS—Cords of truth.

SING—Glorification of the Lord.

SINGING—Affection of the soul for its substance, expressed in tune.

SION—Summit, height, dry place.

SISTER—He who does the will of the Father, another name for spouse or wife.

SIT—To know and understand.

SIX—Truth multiplied by good, or the demonstration of truth in perfected man.

SKILLFUL—Affection of truth, those who unfold from truth by the power of love.

SKIN—Natural man, most external.

SKIRT—Outermost good.

SKULL—Intellect unillumined with truth, that state of darkness which crucifies the Lord.

SLAIN—Separation of all from the divine.

SLAUGHTER—Last judgment.

SLAVE—Those who do not know for themselves.

SLAY—To take the life of.

SLEEP—Awakening to new vision of being, process of self-expansion.

SLUMBER—To doubt, or question.

SMALL AND GREAT—All who worship God.

SMELL—Perceiving truth.

SMITE—Condemn, destroy through ignorance.

SMOKE—Divine truth in ultimates, that which arises from fire or love of truth

SMOOTH—Appertains to truth, quality of truth.

SMYRNA—Myrrh, false doctrines.

SNAKE—Falsehood which comes from judgment by observation.

SNARE—Seduction, falsehood, worldly opinion.

SNOW—Truth in ultimates, whiteness of snow, quality of word made flesh.

SO—In like manner as God.

SOBER—Steadfast and pure, immovable in truth.

SOCKETS OF GOLD—The expansion of good.

SODOM—Burning, self-love.

SOFT—Yielding easily, feminine, receptive to truth.

SOJOURN—To be instructed, proceeding from soul to body.

SOLD—Demonstration of truth in man, the operation of life in unfolding from within out.

SOLDIERS—Keepers of peace, lovers of truth.

SOLES OF THE FEET—Natural principle of man.

SOLICITUDE—Anxiety.

SOLOMON—Perfect, peaceful.

SOLOMON'S TEMPLE—House of wisdom.

SOME—All (truth is indivisible).

SONG—Confession from joy of heart.

SONG OF SOLOMON—Spiritual love.

SON OF GOD—Man made, the image of the Son in the bosom of the Father, the first born, ideal creation.

SON OF MAN—The likeness of the image, the word made flesh, visible body, essential truth of the Lord, true judgment.

SONS—The rise of a new state, from the union of mind and its idea.

SONS AND DAUGHTERS—The truths unfolded from truth are the sons, the love of truth the daughters.

SOOTHSAYERS AND SORCERERS—Those who speak from the world and the love of the world, bearing false witness.

SO-PA-TER—Sacred Father.

SORE—Corrupt state, interior evils, man mortal (Is. 1-6).

SORE AMAZED—Intensely, grievously, painfully.

SORROW—State of worldly opinion as it concerns itself in doing, to bring forth wholeness.

SOSTHENEZ—Saviour, vigorous.

SOUL—Soil, man, the vital principle, being in God, life the gift of God.

SOUND—Vibration of thought, affection of thought.

SOURCE—God, Father, Mother, the source of life, first cause, origin.

SOUTH—Divine light, wisdom, state of being the light is the queen of the south.

SOW—To learn, "sower went forth to sow," man unfolding himself to himse'f.

SPACE—State of consciousness.

SPARE—Save, sanctify.

SPARROW—Spiritual truth.

SPEAK—Perceive and to will, influx of life.

SPEAR—Weapon of spiritual warfare.

SPECKLED — Adulteration, good mixed with evils.

SPEECH—Utterance, expression of mind, demonstration.

SPEED—Living unfoldment of life, operations of soul.

SPENT—Numbered, proven, bestowed.

SPEW OUT—To separate, to eject the false.

SPHERE—The perfect whole, Father-Mother-Son.

SPICES—Interior truths that keep or embalm the body.

SPIDER'S WEB—Treachery of worldy opinions woven together.

SPIES—Those who seek gain through the truth.

SPIKENARD—Perception of truth which is a precious herb.

SPINNING—Thinking from formula, not in natural unfoldment.

SPINE—Substance.

SPIRIT—Life universal, truth and wisdom.

SPIRIT AND THE BRIDE—Heaven and earth, soul and body.

SPIRITUAL BODY—Natural body, the word made flesh, full of grace and truth.

SPIT—Dissolve.

SPITTLE—"Made clay of the spittle, anointing the eyes": signifies bringing the truth of the flesh to the sight of the blind.

SPOIL—To destroy, falsify the truth.

SPOKEN—The Word in action, demonstration of life.

SPONGE—Extreme falsities, that which contains the world's opinions (Matt. 27-48).

SPORT—Worldly delights.

SPOTS—Truth and falsehood, as the world would have it.

SPOUSE—Feminine principle, my idea of myself.

SPREAD—Expand from within out, to multiply.

SPRING—The first state of unfoldment, the same as morning.

SPRINKLE—Glorify with the truth, regeneration.

SQUARE—Perfection.

SQUARING THE CIRCLE—Finding man in God, and God in man.

STAFF—Power, knowledge, support, truth.

STAG (Is. 35: 6)—Joy from the perception of truth.

STAMMERING TONGUE—Those who apprehend truth dimly.

STAND—True judgment from self-evidence, life embodied in fullness.

STAR—Knowledge of truth, the light that lighteth every man, essence of the Lord.

STARS OF HEAVEN—Men of understanding through the Word.

STATE—Being in God, consciousness of life and its unfoldings.

STATUE—Image and likeness, worship of form.

STATUTE—Act of supreme power.

STAVES—Power from truth.

STEAD—Place, order.

STEAL—To judge from the world's standpoint; to deprive man of his divine inheritance.

STEM OF JESSE—Man made, the Lord in His divine humanity.

STEPHANAS, OR STEPHEN—A crown.

STEPS—Ascent from glory to glory, true unfoldment of faith unto faith.

STEWARD—Keeper of the Word, one who is the truth, Jesus Christ.

STICKS—Self-evident truths.

STIFF-NECKED—Proud of self, made from the traditions of men, love of gain and worldly acquirements, unwilling to yield to truth.

STING—Falsehood, subtleties and craftiness of men.

STILL—Truth of being, always, continually.

STINK—Aversion, abomination.

STIR—Action of mind, activity of life, moving of the Holy Spirit.

STOLE—Lawless action of those not in truth, denial of being in God.

STONE—The Lord, natural truth, eternal life.

STONING—Destroying or demolishing, crucifying.

STONY HEART—Love of the world and the ways of the world.

STOOD—Position of man in God, fixed in truth, unwavering faith.

STOOP—To put one's self in power

STOP—Obliterate, deny.

STORE—The good of truth, treasure in heaven.

STORM—Desolation of the world, violent action of mortal belief.

STRAIGHT—I am life, the way and the truth of man.

STRANGERS AND ALIENS—One who does not know himself; unacquainted with life, love and truth.

STRAW—Food of the camel, or the word in the letter, doctrines or scientifics.

STREAM—Influx of truth from the Lord.

STREETS OF GOLD—Ways of God made known in perfect man.

STREETS AND LANES—All ways, everywhere in the living.

STRENGTH—Substance and authority found in self-evidence or faith, the word in the beginning.

STRETCH OUT—Expansion of soul, unfoldment of being, omnipotence.

STRIFE—Seeking worldly gain, discord.

STRIVE—Predicated of the action of truth and love.

STRIKE—Inflict with the words of men.

STRINGED INSTRUMENTS—Affections of truth.

STRIP—To shake off, annihilate.

STRIPES—Inflictions laid upon man by ignorance of truth.

STRONG—The Word of God, powerful, enduring, eternal substance.

STUBBLE—Scientific truth from externals, that which comes from observation, the Word as understood by men, doctrines based in traditions.

STUDY—Unfoldment of man within himself, the law of the Lord revealing itself in man, calling the attention of man from the world.

STUMBLE—Miss the mark of wholeness, fall short of the truth of being.

SUBDUE—Put under, set aside, conquer, soften.

SUBJECT—Placed under, obedient.

SUBSTANCE—Riches of faith, the Kingdom of Heaven.

SUCCOTH—Tents or booths.

SUCH AS—Like unto, equal with, the same, of like substance.

SUCK—Affluence of love, to imbibe truth.

SUCKLINGS—Those who praise and glorify God only in their soul and body.

SUDDENLY—The truth and its action, the coming of light or the Lord.

SUFFER—Allow, permit, let be, that which is in truth.

SUFFICIENT—All, the whole, perfection.

SULPHUR OR BRIMSTONE—Self love, covetousness.

SUMMER—Full state, the same as noon.

SUN—Spiritual love, fire, zeal in truth, the Lord, substance.

SUNRISE—Coming of the Lord.

SUNSET—End of a state of consciousness, blending, evening.

SUP—Explore, "eat of the hidden manna."

SUPPER—Union of God and man, spiritual marriage of soul and body.

SUPPLICATION—True humiliation, realization of the true man.

SURE—Everlasting life.

SUSANNA—A lily, rose or joy.

SWADDLING CLOTHES—Truths of innocence, man the first born.

SWALLOW OR SPARROW—Natural truth.

SWALLOW UP—Exterminate, lose in love.

SWEAR—Confession of truth, living witness in confirmation of being.

SWEAT—Effect of ignorance or denial of truth.

SWEET—Delight of love in itself, the taste of the Lord.

SWELLING—That which pertains to the rising up of fear, from sin as the first cause.

SWIFT—Action of love, instant, or constant, always the same.

SWINE—Getting from the belief of not having, greed, avarice, covetousness.

SWORD—Truth of faith, the Word of God.

SYCAMORE TREE—External church, doctrines of the world, the letter, man in his own self-derived intelligence.

SYMBOLS—Bread and wine of the Holy Supper, chief symbols of man perfected, signs of the Son of man.

SYNAGOGUE—Place of worship, temple of God, soul and body, man.

SIRENE—Opening or key.

SIRIA—Sublime.

T

TABERNACLE—Temple of God, man, soul and body, sanctuary.

TABLE—Instruction, nourishment, table of the Lord is heaven within, external word.

TABLES OF STONE—Two tables of stone upon which is written the law are soul and body, Christ Jesus.

TABRETS—Delights of affection.

TABOR—Purity, contrition, height.

TAIL—The expansion of the head, the ultimate, omega, aggregate, the head and tail are one body; head is faith, the tail confirmation of it.

TAKE AWAY OR TAKEN—Redeeming action, divine omnipotence.

TALE OF THE BRICK—Number of, abundance of.

TALENTS—Good and truth, weight.

TALK—Communion, presence.

TAMAR—Palm tree

TAR AND PITCH—Good mixed with evil, according to the world's way.

TARES—False conceptions, judgment from appearances.

TARRY—To dwell, to imbibe, abide in me, to be as the Lord.

TARSHISH—Trading city.

TARSUS—Winged, feathered.

TASKMASTERS—Those who judge from falsehood, or from traditions of men.

TASTE—Affection of knowledge and understanding, satisfaction of truth.

TAXED—Action of life in man.

TEACH—To impart, unfold, reveal, make manifest.

TEETH—Will and understanding, essentials of mind.

TEAR—Sign of the operations of truth unto resurrection from the dead; Jesus wept at the grave of Lazarus.

TEKEL—Weighed.

TEKOA—Tent pitching.

TELL—Communication, unfold, truth in the ultimate.

TEMAN OR TEMA—Desert, perfect.

TEMPEST—Action of truth upon error, disturbance of the world's opinions by the influx of truth.

TEMPLE—The Lord in human form, the body.

TEMPT—Provoke to unfoldment, to call forth, urge, to try, or incite.

TEN—All things, what is full, heaven and earth, totality.

TENT—Holy things of love, place of worship of the ancient. Holy man, the Lord called a tent.

TENDER—Opening of truth, genuine faith in its first inception.

TENTH PART—The same as ten, perfect whole.

TERAPHIM—Idols appealed to when they consulted with God.

TERROR—Absence from God, separation from life.

TESTAMENT—Living statement, witness of truth, I am life.

TESTIMONY—Divine truth, the word made flesh.

THADDAEUS—Praising.

THANKSGIVING — Acknowledgment and glorification of the Lord.

THEE—Perfected man, the Lord.

THIEF—Silent force operating in man to remove evil. (Rev. 3-3.)

THIEF—From the false view, is man who robs himself of eternal life, man (a den of thieves).

THEN—Now, at this time.

THEM—Traditions of men, worldly beliefs, falsehood.

THEOPHILUS—Friend of God, lover of God.

THERE—Within and without, in man, state of being.

THESSALONICA—Victory.

THIGH—Fundamental love.

THIN—Without truth and faith.

THINGS—Visible creation, universe, that which is brought forth from substance.

THINK—Action of mind, natural moving of the Spirit.

THIRD DAY—What is full, resurrection unto life, beginning of sanctification.

THIRST—Realization of fullness, blessedness, immortality.

THIRTEEN—Compound of ten and three, state of remaining, or eternal state.

THIRTY—The reign of righteousness in man, the beginning of combat.

THIS—Man as he is, soul and body.

THISTLES—Curse and devastation, falsehood.

THOMAS—Twin.

THORNS—Self-love, self-righteousness, prickles from opinions of men.

THOUGHT—Vibration of mind produced by love of being.

THOUSAND—Much, innumerable, indefinite quantity, what is eternal.

THREE—What is full and complete from beginning to end.

THREE MEN—Son in the bosom of the Father, Son of God and the Son of man, the living witness.

THRESH—Separate truth from error, dissipate darkness with light.

THRESHING FLOOR—Where the good of truth is, or the working out of life in its expansion.

THRUST—Violent and all-powerful action of silence, life truth, when man yields to its power.

THROAT AND TONGUE—Conjunction between the invisible and visible, or the within and without, tongue, two-edged sword.

THRONE—Man, judgment, heaven, authority, power, seat of the King.

THROUGH—The state of reception of truth.

THUMB—Fullness of intelligence externally written.

THUMMEN AND URIM—Soul and body; fire and brightness thereof, the stone that reveals all mysteries, Christ Jesus.

THUNDER—Voice of life, truth and love, all pervading presence, power and knowledge.

THYATIRA—Perfume, scent.

TIGERS—Fierce animal love, type of affection of the world.

TILL THE GROUND—Cultivate the soil or soul by love of faith or soul substance.

TIMBREL AND HARP—Truth and good in demonstration.

TIME—Now, state of conscious being, eternal life.

TIME NO MORE—(Rev. 10-6)—No division in man, as birth and death, no separation in soul and body.

TIME, TIMES AND A HALF A TIME—The same as one thousand, two hundred and sixty days, from substance to substance, or from seed to seed.

TIMOTHEUS OR TIMOTHY—Honored by God.

TIN—Natural man.

TIRZAH—Beautiful, benevolent, well pleasing.

TITHES—All; good and truth stored up in man remain, the real and everlasting man.

TITTLE—Word, the least which is the greatest.

TITUS—Honorable.

TO-DAY—What is eternal and perpetual, state of being in the Lord.

TOBIAH—Goodness of God.

TOKEN—The presence of the Lord, remembered in what I am, or in what man is.

TOE—Understanding in its ultimate use.

TOGETHER—At-one-ment, agreement, unity, collect to one body, gather with the Lord.

TOLD—Made known.

TOMB—Man's false belief of himself, the measure of darkness.

TO-MORROW—Eternity, to-day and yesterday.

TONGS—Purifiers, truths.

TONGUE—Sword, doctrine, Word of God, servant of the heart.

TOOK—Assimilate, appropriate, bring into remembrance.

TOOL—Thought and word.

TOP—The truth of faith, dawning of light is the top of the mountains.

TOPAZ—Good of celestial love.

TOPHET—Darkness, ignorance.

TORCH—Love of truth.

TORMENT—Stupid, dormant understanding, self-love, love of the world.

TORN—Belief of separation, that which pertains to death.

TOSSED—Buffeted by falsehood, wavering through doubt.

TOUCH—Affection of good, conjunction by communication.

TOWARD—Signifies in, or the presence of.

TOWEL—Divine truth.

TOWER—Man in God, build a tower is to be eternal life.

TOWN—Possession, a state of being.

TRADE—Exchange of opinions, agreement to doctrines, procuring or acquiring truths from others.

TRADITIONS—Hearsay from men of all states and ages of belief, generations of commands from the world concerning man.

TRAMPLE—Destroy by falsehood.

TRANCE—Insensibility.

TRANQUILITY—Harmony in truth, internal peace.

TRANSFIGURATION—Fullness from the Lord, through seeing man is the "Beloved Son."

TRANSGRESSION—Missing the mark of wholeness, or declaring against man as the substance of the Father.

TRAVAIL—Change of state in the unfolding of the within out.

TREAD—Explore, examine myself or the works of God which are manifested in man.

TREASURE—The Word of God, book of life, man in God, knowledge of Jesus Christ.

TREE—Man rooted in God is the tree of life, will and understanding the trunk of the tree, words and acts the leaves, blossoms, fruit.

TREMBLE—Change of state preceding the coming of truth in its fullness.

TRESPASS—Going away from truth.

TRIBES, TWELVE—Truths of faith.

TRIBULATION—Travail in bringing forth truth.

TRIBUTE OR CUSTOM—They who serve in the freedom of the truth, confession of truth.

TRIED—Proven by fire, cleansed, made fit for use.

TRINITY—Father, Mother, Son, the Divine essence in one man; life, love, truth; fire, light, heat; Word, Word, Word. (John 1-1). God, heaven, earth, the beginning.

TRODDEN—Denial of truth, rejection of Christ. (Luke 8-5.)

TROOP OR DROVE—Omnipotence, omniscience, omnipresence, the good of faith, or divine intelligence.

TROUBLE—The effort to bring forth truth.

TRUE—Self-evident, real, alive unto life eternal, the nature of perfect man.

TRULY—Verily, amen, the living One.

TRUMPET—Revelation, the call of God in man, proceeding of the spirit of life in awakening man from sleep.

TRUST—The trust of the Lord is faith in Himself, rest in self-evidence or living substance.

TRUTH—The Lord, man in dominion and power over all flesh, Son of man glorified.

TRUTH OF GOOD—Denotes the masculine, the good of truth the feminine, the same as truth and wisdom, or will and understanding.

TUBAL CAIN—Doctrine of natural man.

TUMULT—Desire, covetousness, eagerness to gain, haste to become whole or perfect.

TURBAN—Intelligence of truth.

TURN—To will and to do.

TURN ASIDE—Judgment, pervert and destroy.

TURTLE DOVES AND YOUNG PIGEONS—Offering of that which is, the type of the first born, spiritual birth.

TWAIN—Father, Mother, externalized in man, woman, one perfect son, soul and body.

TWELVE—All things of faith, knowledge in chief; twelve gates, perfect power; twelve stones, everlasting substance.

TWELVE—Twelve disciples, activities of life; twelve sons, complete demonstration of man's possibilities.

TWENTY—Compounded of twice ten, superior degree of truth, state of perfect unfoldment.

TWILIGHT—Blending of day and night, or God and man, the last time.

TWINS—Conceived together, good and truth.

TWO OLIVE TREES—The expansion of one, the same as six, marriage from faith, the witnesses in earth of the record in heaven.

TYRE—Rock, strength.

U

U—Means a sound of affection.

ULTIMATE—The whole, the body, the word made flesh.

UNAWARES—Unlooked for, suddenly, in the twinkling of an eye.

UNBELIEF—Ignorance of truth, unwillingness to receive the light.

UNCIRCUMCISED—Those who have not cut off from them the world's beliefs and opinions.

UNCLEAN—In the world's way of being, not whole, imperfect, adulterated.

UNCLOTHED—Without the garments of righteousness.

UNCOVER—The action of life, truth and love.

UNCTION—Power from the Holy Spirit, realization of love, knowledge of the Lord.

UNDEFILED—Holy, pure, harmless, perfect, untouched by sin.

UNDER—In agreement with, in at-one-ment.

UNDERSTANDING — Acknowledgment of truth, in the faith of God, chief faculty of man.

UNFRUITFUL—Rich in the ways and works of the world.

UNGODLY—Not in the truth, lovers of the world.

UNICORN—Falsehood.

UNITE—Action of truth in man.

UNION—Perpetual state of God and man.

UNITY—The reciprocal union of the Father, Mother, Son.

UNIVERSE—One made manifest by love.

UNJUST—Not equal, not at one with truth, untrue to self and untrue to God.

UNPROFITABLE — Idle, worthless, that which brings forth nothing.

UNRIGHTEOUS—Not right from the standpoint of God.

UNSEARCHABLE — Past human understanding, beyond man's realm of thought.

UNSPEAKABLE—Inmost, soul language, love of God.

UNSPOTTED—Pure, perfect, holy.

UPHAZ—Finest gold.

UPHOLD—Power of truth, knowledge of being.

UPPER—The spirit of love and life, state of holiness.

UPRIGHT—The way of God in creation.

URIAH—The light of God.

URIM—The light that lighteth every man, the love of God, the fire or zeal of life, judgment in truth.

US—Father, Mother, Son.

USE—Appropriate, acknowledge, bring forth unto perfection.

USURY—One who works for reward, or does good for the sake of gain.

UTTER—Declare, make known, unfold, reveal.

UTTERLY — Completely, totally, without limit.

UTTERMOST—To the extreme, to the end in the beginning.

UZ—Fruitful land, counsel, or wood.

UZZIAH—Strength.

UZZIEL—Strength of God.

V

VAGABOND—That which has no knowledge of truth and good.

VAIL—Appearance, form, word made flesh; entrance into the Holiest, passage to the essential divine.

VAIN—Falsity of doctrine, foolish, unprofitable, blasphemous.

VALLEY—The spoken word, the fruitful valley is man in truth and good, understanding.

VALOR—Strength, wisdom, virtue, knowledge.

VASHTI—The world's idea of man.

VAPOR—Ultimate truth of love.

VENGEANCE—The action of truth upon all less than itself.

VENISON—Truth of the natural from whence comes the good of life.

VERILY—Amen, let it be, the oath of Jesus.

VERY—Only true and living.

VESSEL—Man; chosen vessel, man of God.

VESTURE—The word made flesh, holy substance interwoven in body.

VEXATION—Traditions of men, falsehood, worldly beliefs.

VIALS—Cup or measure of truth which destroys error, "full of wrath" is full of love.

VICTORY—Eternal life, man of God, the gift of God.

VICTUALS—Bread and wine, that which sustains life is "I am life." (John 6-48.)

VIEW—To know the truth.

VILLAGES—Doctr'nes, truths col ected from various sources.

VILE—Imperfect, unholy, impure, corrupt.

VINE—"I am the real vine," man born of God.

VINEYARD—The universe, the church of God.

VINE-DRESSERS—Those who are in truths and teach them.

VINEGAR AND GALL—Good and evil.

VIOLENCE—Adulteration of truth.

VIPER—Mortal hatred, deceitful doctrines, sophistry.

VIRGIN—Man-woman, the Immortal One, image of the Father-Mother, God as man, the Christ, the divine idea unfolded or revealed.

VIRTUE—Strength, life, power, man in truth, the Lord.

VISION—Inmost revelation.

VISIT—Denotes the living presence seen and acknowledged.

VOICE—What is announced from the spirit of life, the Divine Word, influx of truth.

VOID—Nothing seen or known except by hearsay, no self-evidence.

VOLUME OR ROLL—Quality of being life, God's Word, man the book written by the finger of God.

VOW—The will of God confirmed in man.

W

WAFERS—Spiritual good, miraculous food, type of living bread.

WAGES—Eternal life, true reward, the gift of God, death to falsehood.

WAGGING—Action of self-derived intelligence.

WAGONS—Knowledges and doctrines from appearances.

WAILING—Effect of bringing forth from false premise, or from error.

WAIT—Rest in stillness, cease striving to do and get.

WALK—To unfold by faith or self-evidence, to live in truth, to act from being life, truth, and love.

WALLET—Natural man.

WALLOW—Floundering in the world's discord. the mire of self-love.

WALLS—Truth in ultimates. salvation in the Word of God embodied by man.

WANDER—To look outside of truth, to judge by appearances only.

WANT—Desire from ignorance, lack of understanding.

WAR—Combat with ignorance, conflict of light and darkness.

WAR IN HEAVEN—(Rev. 12-7)—The love of God or the wrath of God in its true judgment, by which all things are made new.

WARD—State of false belief relative to imprisonment.

WARM—Affection of truth.

WAS—New state, eternal life, man as he is

WASH—Purify, regenerate, baptism signifies spiritual birth. (John 13: 8-9.)

WASTE — Devastate, to make desolate through ignorance, belief of separation.

WATCH—Concentrate all forces upon the truth.

WATCH-TOWER—Man in the knowledge of himself as he is in God.

WATER—Truth; cold water, obedience to truth because of truth.

WATER AND SPIRIT—To be born of water is to be born of truth, and of spirit is to be filled with the power of truth.

WAVE—Life flowing in by the acknowledgment of life.

WAX AND MYRRH—Preservation of the body, types of truths which embalm.

WAY—That which is made ready, "I am the way," that already prepared, the "highway" is being as the Father is.

WE—Father, Mother, Son; "I and my Father."

WEAK—Ignorant, subject to the world.

WEALTH—Knowledge of the Kingdom of Heaven as embodied in Christ Jesus, the only true living man.

WEAN—Separation from truth.

WEAPONS—Self-evidence, "rod and staff," soul and body, man in truth.

WEARY—State of longing for rest or the Lord's presence, combat with the world.

WEAVE—To teach from conviction, self-evidence.

WEBS—False doctrines.

WEDDING GARMENT—Divine truth from the Lord, living body, eternal life, the gift of God.

WEEK—Holy state, period of seven days, equal to one day, regeneration, and reformation in which man rests.

WEEP—"Jesus wept," effort to unfold life into life, in the midst of conflicting beliefs.

WEEPING—"Mary weeping" means love in its power to bring forth truth, the action of love.

WELL OF LIVING WATER—Depth of understanding of eternal life.

WEIGH—The estimate of truth within itself.

WELL BELOVED—Loved in truth, loved by God, loved unto perfection and holiness.

WENT—Action of truth in all ways.

WEPT—Intensity of love in demonstration of itself in the midst of the adversary.

WEST—Evening, blending.

WHALE—"As in Adam all die," a tpye of the natural man.

WHEAT—Seed of God, spiritual man, perfect substance.

WHEAT AND "TARES"—Real and unreal, truth and error, man from the world's view, and man from God's view of him.

WHEELS—Power of proceeding, faculty of reasoning, action of mind, thought.

WHELP OF A LION—Affirmation and acknowledgment of truth.

WHIRLWIND—Power of the Spirit which lifts within itself man.

WHISPER—False belief of separation, absence from truth, fear.

WHITE—Intelligence, purity, light of the world, man in God.

WHITE STONE—Christ Jesus, the Lord, truth of being which the builders reject.

WHO IS, WAS, AND WILL BE—I am, man as he is in reality.

WHOLE—Complete, perfect, finished work of God, life and the body.

WHOREDOM—Adulterate and falsify the truth, belief of separation from God, union with many falsehoods.

WILL—Mother, soul, essential principle, love,

WIDOW—One without protection or provision by God, the world's idea of men; soul and body not saved is without a husband.

WIFE—God's divine, holy idea of Himself made manifest as man, and unfolded from man unto himself as help suitable (the only help); God perfects Himself in man, so man perfects himself in man-female (or Christ Jesus our Lord).

WICKED—Removed from truth, state of falsification from the world's beliefs, traditions of the fathers, declarations of men.

WILDERNESS—Secret place, interior possibilities, hidden man, the uncreate, spontaneous unfolding of the natural man, where old things pass away and all things become new.

WILLOWS—Spontaneous growth by the waters of life, obedient, yielding thoughts in truth.

WIND—Breath of God, Holy Spirit, action of life, power of self-evidence acting in man.

WINE—Blood of life, vital principle shed or made visible in the true communion, spiritual drink.

WINE PRESS—Exploration and examination of "I am," chemical analysis from principle, or divine light, the true and only proving.

WINDOW—Influx of light, outlook from and towards truth, spiritual perception.

WINGS—Power and defense, omnipresence and omniscience, "with twain he covered his face," love and wisdom.

WINTER—The same as night, sleep, obscurity.

WIPE AWAY—To take away by the power of truth.

WISDOM—Justice and judgment of truth, right use of knowledge, that which receives of God and makes manifest from God.

WISE—Those who embody eternal life, those who are equal with the Father, those who shine with the light of life.

WISH—Desire, prophet of that which is.

WITCH—Falsity of self-love.

WITHER—To become powerless, to go away from life, without substance.

WITHIN—Essential essence, the all in all, the within and without are one.

WITNESS—Acknowledgment in presence and person, confession of truth, confirmation of being.

WIZARDS — The falsification of truth through self-love.

WOE—Alas, exclamation of lamentation, state of those out of truth.

WOLF—That which seizes and gathers spoil, that which preys upon and snatches with greed or avidity.

WOMAN—Man's highest unfoldment, the "Blessed Virgin," that which makes alive; it is not good for man to be alone, without the life-giving spirit or woman.

WOMB—Where truth and life is conceived, corresponds to love in man; conjunction of good and truth.

WONDER—Surprise, delight at the operation of faith.

WONDERFUL—The name of the Son of God, character of man in perfection, not commonly recognized.

WOOD—The good that belongs to works, to cut wood is to place merit in doing.

WOOL—The good of love, the externalization of good, as in the radiation from the sheep.

WORD—Man, the Lord, divine truth, life, light.

WORK OF GOD—Man, which includes all things, the sent of God, Christ Jesus.

WORLD—People of God; the world also means the false beliefs of men taken as a whole.

WORM—Finite, mortal conception of man.

WORMWOOD—The state of bitterness of man rooted in his own self-derived opinion.

WORSHIP—Exaltation of the Lord, realization of the love of God as found in true being.

WORTHY—To realize power from the standpoint of truth, merit, grace, favor of man in God.

WOUNDED—Disagreement with the Lord.

WRATH OF GOD—The love of God, judgment of God, light of truth.

WRESTLING—Temptation, combat of man in self-unfoldment, travail of the soul.

WRETCHED—Incoherent, uncertain, doubtful.

WRITE—To commit to God spirit, soul and body, to implant in the life the truth of being, to impress the truth in love.

WROTH—State of activity of the spirit in moving upon the face of the waters.

WROUGHT—Intwined, interwoven, blending of God and man, finished work of God in creation.

Y

YE—Man.

YEA—Amen, verily, I am.

YEAR—Full time, entire, beginning and end, what is eternal, Kingdom of Heaven, state of blessedness, or judgment.

YELLOW—The color of good, glory, sunlight, rest.

YESTERDAY—Eternity, now.

YET—Hitherto, relates to now.

YIELD—Submit, produce, unfold from truth.

YOKE—That which unites or binds two in one, eternal life, the yoke of Christ, at-one-ment.

YONDER—In the bosom of the Father, rest in being as the Father is.

YOU—Man, the living Word of God.

YOUNG—Affection of the church or man for truth.

YOUTH—Beginning in God.

Z

ZACCHEUS—Pure, clean, just, innocent.

ZACHARIAH—Remembered by Jehovah.

ZADOCK—Just, justified.

ZALMUNNA—Shadow, image.

ZARAH—East, brightness.

ZEBEDEE—Abundant portion given of God.

ZAREPHATH—One desiring truth, widow.

ZEAL—Love of God, intensity of truth.

ZEBULUM—Dwelling, habitation, heavenly marriage.

ZEDEKIAH—Justice of Jehovah, truth itself.

ZELOTES—Full of zeal.

ZENAS—I live, living.

ZEPHANIAH—Secret of the Lord, treasure of the Lord.

ZERUBBABEL—Represents the Lord born in Babylon.

ZIDON—External worship.

ZIKLAG—Measure.

ZIMRI—My field, my branch.

ZION—Man in the highest sense, the glory of God, the Lord.

ZIPPORAH—Beauty, crown, quality of the external church.

ZIZ—Flower, wing, feather, branch.

ZONE—Common band or belt, which unites or holds.

www.ingramcontent.com/pod-product-compliance
Lightning Source LLC
Chambersburg PA
CBHW020857230426
43666CB00008B/1223